Jardine

cooking with an accent

Enjoy the Book

[signature]

GEORGE JARDINE

Edited and photographed by Russel Wasserfall
Art directed and designed by Roxy Spears

Preface

How did I get here? Well, it has certainly been a winding road with lots of twists and turns and lots of great people along the way. I am George Jardine, I was born in Edinburgh, Scotland in 1972. I lived there for 18 years almost exactly to the day and then I began my journey. I migrated to the south of England and worked with a great chef, Tommy Gordon, who grounded me and set me on the right track in my career.

After a bit of wandering, I ended up at the Four Seasons on Park Lane with Jean Christophe Novelli. It was through this relationship that I ended up on South African shores at the Cellars Hohenort with Liz McGrath when I was offered a position as executive chef there. Five magical years in Cape Town followed, mainly because I met my wife Louise le Riche, who proceeded to introduce me to all of the wonders of South Africa.

In 2001 we moved to Indonesia where Dharmawangsa Hotel in Jakarta was our home for 12 months of luxury. Then we moved to Malaysia, living in Kuala Lumpur for four years where I worked at the Shangri-La Hotel and Louise wrote for a few local magazines. Life was good and out popped two little boys, William and Louis. Malaysia was fantastic – the people were awesome and the food was delicious, but we knew Cape Town was home, and constantly discussed plans to come back.

As we were about to up-root and leave, the Shangri-La group bought their first property outside of Asia in Sydney, Australia. They asked me to go and open the property, a big opportunity and too good to turn down. Cape Town would have to wait a little longer, and Sydney became home for two years.

Finally, in 2006, we made it home to our first love – Cape Town. I set up a restaurant on Bree Street in the CBD with an old friend, Willem Kuhn, and it proved to be reasonably successful for four years. Then, as the boys got older, we decided to move to Stellenbosch, where we met Gary and Kathy Jordan and discussed opening a restaurant in a little piece of heaven called Jordan Estate. The boys now walk to school barefoot and here I am telling you this story.

What I've learnt, and what has shaped my life in every country and every restaurant in which I have worked, is just how valuable the people are that you meet along the way. The locals, the chefs, waiters, scullers, managers, the old guy sitting at the bar; these are the people who know where the best food is, where the fat galjoen are, the secret spots for porcini, the best things to do. I have invested my whole life in relationships, because if you put the effort in, you get the best out.

It kind of works like that with your relationship with a restaurant too. If you build a relationship with a restaurant, its people, its menu, you can get the best out of it. If you understand where the chef is coming from, or why he gets excited about this shellfish or that cheese, you can learn which of his dishes will give you the best eating experience. If you just pop in there once, your experience will only ever be a flash in the pan. That's also why I work so hard at building relationships with producers and suppliers; I want to understand them so I can get the best out of them.

We are purveyors, and that is why produce is vital to our craft. A restaurant is only as good as the produce it sells, our dishes are simply a means to showcase something that is naturally beautiful, our seasonings enhance the natural flavours and we shouldn't need to season to mask an inferior product. Unfortunately all too often things are not all they seem to be – a carrot can be modified to be orange and grow straight, animals are pumped full of growth hormones and chemicals to make them get fat quickly. The ocean is dredged clean of all life to fill supermarket freezers with fish fingers. Who eats that stuff anyway and what fish is it exactly? The variety of SASSI green-listed fish becomes less and less every year, and soon farmed fish may be our only option.

We have all seen the tragic photos of commercially farmed animals. They're not good. I want to know that what is going into my mouth is healthy, sustainable and as natural as possible. So this is why we make so much effort in sourcing our produce and why I want to celebrate and elevate the small producers that are taking care to look after us. You may pay a little more for this knowledge, but you can eat safely knowing that it's all natural.

What really matters to me, and what I would like to get across in this book, is the importance of building relationships in order to get the best end product, and of course the best journey in finding that product. But the relationship is not just with other people. I think it is vital to build a relationship with your environment, walk in the forest and see what is growing between the trees or on the side of the road.

Growing vegetables or fruit, and understanding the seasons and seasonal produce are all very important. When something is in season, it will be at its best – and that's when I want to eat it. The fish you buy in a small fishing town straight off the boat may be the same fish as in the supermarket, but it tastes better because you've seen the boat, you've chatted to the fishermen, you've smelt the sea air and you've started to create a relationship with your food source.

My best food memories are not necessarily from the great restaurants I have eaten in. I remember digging up new potatoes with my mum for Sunday lunch, simply boiling them and eating them with butter, or picking brambles and elderberries with my sister and cousins. We used to pick buckets full, then eat them until our faces were bright red. My grandmother would make jam with the ones not consumed and wine with the elderberries.

I love meeting people like the ones mentioned in this book: Sue Baker, Ryan Boon and Wayne Rademeyer who share a passion for, and care about, what we consume. Wayne's mozzarella is the best in the world for me because of this association – I know exactly where it comes from and the level of care and love taken to produce it. The restaurant is the same – we know our regulars on a first-name basis, we chat as if we are old friends, they get the best experience from the restaurant because each party has put effort in. They put in the effort to come in the first place, they get to know the waiters and chat to the chefs, and our effort and part of this relationship is to give them the best experience we can.

During this process we have asked our friends, good customers and family to try out our recipes. We couldn't put a recipe book together without knowing if they could be reproduced in a home kitchen. Some efforts have been very successful and some needed a few goes to get them right. The feedback was fantastic. Amazingly all the recipe testers attempted the dishes without the photos as reference. This is admirable, or maybe it's a sign that the recipes work.

Thanks to all the testers for their work, understanding and patience.

Bernadine van Zyl

Carina Fourie

Ilse Lombaard

Maryna de Kock

Nicola and Rachel Theron

Nic Oosthuizen

Nina le Riche

Contents

Eggs

As a chef, I believe that the best reason for using good produce is that you get a better end product from it. Many different factors define good produce, including how it's grown and where. This shouldn't be news; we are bombarded in the media about sustainable food and good food journeys. You can hardly have missed the whole organic revolution.

These days there's free-range or grass-fed this and pasture-reared that. Line-caught fish distinguishes fish that had a chance from some poor creature scooped up in a trawl-net along with every other ocean-going animal for miles. We are all aware of the importance of treading softly on the planet and harvesting our needs from it in a sustainable way.

I think that often the best produce choice is not only about what it looks like, but also how it was grown or raised. I don't want to be serving something that arrived at the door after being genetically modified, grown in chemical fertiliser or condemned to a miserable life.

Which brings us to eggs. Using an egg produced by a happy, healthy hen makes all the difference in my cooking. We get our fresh eggs twice a week from a farm called Homegrown. The chickens are free to walk around and enjoy a life of scratching and cackling, and occasionally laying an egg.

Free-range is a bit of a catch-phrase for eggs these days, especially since the big retailers have seen it as a great marketing opportunity. As with many things, there are degrees. Homegrown is a truly wholesome operation run by people who love their chickens. If you are as concerned about the source of your food as I am, take the time to visit the farm or the producer and find some lovely people to do business with. Take your kids and show them the circle of life; you can even sing the song from Lion King in the car on the way back.

Poached Hen's Egg Soup

Once you have made the soup, you can place it in a cream gun (if you have one) to give it a very light mousse consistency. If you don't have one, then just serve it chilled – both ways are delicious.

Soup

1 small bunch of leeks,
    finely chopped and washed
1 large potato, diced
3 cloves garlic, crushed
1 litre chicken stock
50 ml cream
salt and pepper to taste

In a large pot gently sweat off the leeks over low heat so as not to colour during the process – you just want them to cook gently.

Add the potato, garlic and chicken stock and cook until the potato is soft.

Blend this until smooth, strain through a sieve and chill. Once chilled, add the cream and season with salt and pepper.

Herb Crust

50 g Parmesan
20 g breadcrumbs
50 g butter
10 g parsley
10 g basil
100 g watercress

Blend the Parmesan, breadcrumbs, butter, parsley and basil into a fine paste.

Spread this mixture between 2 sheets of greaseproof paper and chill. Once chilled, cut into rectangles big enough to cover each egg.

1 egg per person

Poach the eggs, keeping them nice and soft. Dry them slightly with kitchen paper.

Cover each egg with the herb crust and place under a hot grill to melt.

Serve the soup ice cold with an egg in the middle and garnish with the watercress.

Serves 4

Baked Truffled Egg

Tarts

200 g butter puff pastry
25 g prosciutto
4 eggs

Preheat the oven to 180°C.

Roll out the puff pastry to 50-mm-thick sheets.

Cut this sheet into discs twice as big as the moulds you are using (we use a normal silicon cupcake tray).

Place the pastry into the moulds, making sure there are no air pockets.

Line each mould with prosciutto and then crack one egg into each tart. This should fill to the top of the pastry.

Bake in the oven for 12 minutes until the egg is cooked but still soft in the middle.

Hollandaise Sauce

250 g butter
50 ml white wine vinegar
2 black peppercorns
1 shallot, chopped
4 eggs
10 g fresh truffle, chopped
   (or truffle oil to taste)
salt and pepper to taste

Put the butter in a small pot and heat gently until clarified.

Reduce the white wine vinegar, peppercorns and shallot by half. Strain this reduction.

Separate 4 eggs, place the yolks in a bowl and add the vinegar reduction. Whisk over a double boiler until cooked. It should be smooth ribbon stage not scrambled.

Remove from heat and slowly add the clarified butter, whisking continuously until thickened. If needed, add a little warm water to thin down.

Add the chopped truffle and season with salt and pepper.

Spoon over the tarts, grill until golden brown and serve.

Makes 4 tarts

Honey & Poppy Seed Soufflé

Soufflé Base

6 egg yolks
50 g castor sugar
20 g cake flour
250 ml milk
5 ml honey
2 g poppy seeds

In a large bowl, combine the egg yolks, castor sugar and flour.

Bring the milk to the boil. Pour it over the egg mixture, whisking to combine quickly.

Return this mixture to the pot and cook over a low heat until it thickens to a paste. Stir continuously. Do not let this mixture boil, but make sure the flour is cooked out for at least 5 minutes.

Once it has thickened, remove from the heat, mix in the honey and poppy seeds and chill as quickly as possible.

Soufflé

50 g soufflé base
10 g soft butter
20 g brown sugar
100 g egg white
30 g sugar

Preheat the oven to 180°C.

Brush 2x13cm ramekins or moulds evenly with the soft butter. Place in a fridge to set slightly, then brush again with butter. Coat the buttered moulds with the brown sugar, making sure there are no gaps.

In a large bowl whisk the egg whites with the sugar until you have formed semi-stiff peaks. Fold the whites into the base mixture, making sure it is well incorporated but do not overmix.

Pour the mixture into the two moulds. Scrape off the top with a palette knife to make it even and clean any excess mix off the moulds.

Place the soufflé into the oven and bake for 10 minutes. Serve immediately.

Serves 4

Poached Duck Egg

This is quick to prepare and makes a great starter if you are serving a light main meal.

Polenta

500 ml chicken stock
100 g instant polenta
100 g butter
50 g Parmesan

Bring the chicken stock to the boil and add the polenta, whisking until it thickens (it should be like porridge).

Slowly add the butter and Parmesan (it should become creamy and have a texture like good mashed potato).

200 g washed rind
  Taleggio cheese
30 ml cream
salt and pepper to taste

In a pan slowly melt the Taleggio with the cream and season with the salt and pepper.

1 duck egg per person

Poach the duck egg in gently boiling water with a little vinegar. Use a small blowtorch to brown the top.

This is great with watercress or rocket to break the richness.

Serves 4

Steamed Asparagus

It is always a happy time when the new season's asparagus arrives. Asparagus is a very versatile ingredient that can be used in many ways. This is a great early summer starter or lunch dish, and it's quick and easy to make. My mum always used to give us chopped egg for breakfast with a little knob of butter and salt and pepper. I have just used her idea and turned it into a dressing.

1 egg
1 bunch of asparagus
sliced pancetta
5 g chopped parsley
30 ml olive oil
5 ml sherry vinegar
salt and pepper to taste

Boil some water in a pot with a little salt, add the egg and boil for 5 minutes. Remove the shell and leave to cool slightly.

Place the asparagus in the boiling water and cook for 30 seconds. Remove and dress with a little olive oil.

Set your oven to grill and cook the pancetta until crispy.

Chop the egg and place into a bowl with the parsley, olive oil and vinegar. Season with salt and pepper.

Arrange the asparagus on a plate, spoon over the egg dressing and top with the crispy pancetta.

You can eat this as is or with some dressed watercress or rocket.

Serves 2

Fish

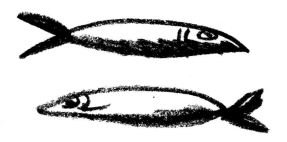

When my father-in-law Louis le Riche retired from his law practice in Bredasdorp and moved to the nearby coastal village of Struisbaai, it followed that the family would spend a lot of time there. Struisbaai pretty much typifies why I love this country so much. Where else in the world is there such natural beauty, combined with the infrastructure you need daily, as well as the bounty of the ocean right on your doorstep?

For my sons, holidays at the beach house in Struisbaai are a kind of *Boy's Own* adventure. They go fishing with me and their grandad, and there's plenty of space to run and play. If the wind's too strong for fishing, they can always fly kites or ride bicycles in perfect safety. It's idyllic.

Louis is a keen fisherman, with an incredible knowledge of the species he targets and the environment in which they occur. He has opened my eyes to different kinds of fishing and sustainability, noting the change from slow old *tjakkies* (which did 5 to 6 knots and fished close to shore), to ski boats which are faster and can hunt fish up to 100 kilometres out.

A lot of the knowledge in preparation and cleaning that Louis has passed on to me as we tackle the fishing spots near the Le Riche home is applied in the restaurant. Louise sometimes says that I married her just so I could spend time with her father. It's true, we do get on famously and have a great time fishing together, but maybe it was the fishing that got me hooked in the first place. Much of what we catch is released, but species that aren't on the SASSI watch list occasionally end up on a dinner plate.

When it comes to the restaurant, we can't always get line-caught fish, but we have developed excellent sources of local, sustainably farmed or fresh-caught species. A lot of it comes from the commercial fishing operations in Struisbaai. I pop into the local fish shop whenever I'm there for a look at what's in season and what might make a nice meal.

Steamed East Coast Hake, Young Beets, Apple & Smoked Mussels

We get fantastic hake in South Africa, mostly from the East Coast near Mossel Bay. The hake industry is sustainable so it gets a green status from SASSI. This is very important to us all and we only use sustainably farmed or harvested produce.

Hake

800 g hake fillet
20 g flat-leaf parsley
1 egg white
500 ml cream
salt and pepper to taste
olive oil

Trim the hake into 4 portions – each should be 150 g.

Place the remaining 200 g of trimmings into a blender and blend with the parsley until smooth. Add the egg white and 200 ml of the cream and blend on a pulse setting until it is fully incorporated. Do not over-mix it once the cream has been added.

Season with salt and pepper.

Lay out a sheet of plastic wrap, brush with olive oil and spread out a layer of the hake mousse the same width as the hake fillet and twice as long.

Place the hake in the middle and wrap it up.
Chill until needed.

When required, steam for 5 minutes until cooked.

Mussel Velouté

2 chopped shallots
1 clove garlic, crushed
1 glass white wine
250 g mussels
200ml fish stock

Sweat the chopped shallot and crushed garlic in a large pot. Add the white wine and mussels and steam until they are just open.

Remove the flesh from the mussels and reserve. Now strain off the juice and return it to the pot with the fish stock, reduce this by half then add the remainder of the cream (300 ml) and reduce until silky smooth.

Beets

3 baby beets per portion
parsley, chopped

Roast the beets in a tin foil bag in the oven. This will take 30–40 minutes. Peel while still hot as it is much easier.

Add the mussels to the velouté and spoon generously over the hake.

Arrange the beets around the hake and garnish with some chopped parsley.

Serves 4

Fried Snoek Kuite, Aromatic Curried Lentils, Apple & Mint

Maybe my favourite thing to do with snoek is on a braai with some apricot jam, but fried kuite (roe) fresh from a fat snoek from the West Coast comes pretty close to my favourite.

Curried Lentils

1 large onion
50 ml vegetable oil
6 cloves garlic
1 stick lemongrass
2 chillies
10 g cardamom
10 g star anise
10 g black peppercorns
5 g coriander seeds
1 tin of tomatoes
100 g brown lentils
500 ml fish stock
50 g butter
salt and pepper to taste

Peel and roughly chop the onion. Place it in a blender with the oil, garlic, lemongrass and chilli and blend to a smooth paste.

Heat a heavy-bottomed pan and gentle sauté the paste until caramelised.

Toast the spices in a non-stick pan to release the oils and blend to a powder.

Add spices to the onion mix and cook for a further 2 minutes. Then add the tin of tomatoes and cook until almost dry. Add the lentils and fish stock and cook gently until the lentils are cooked.

Finish by gradually adding the butter and season with salt and pepper. The end result should be saucy, aromatic and slightly spicy.

Beer Batter

100 g cake flour
1 x 375ml bottle beer
200 g snoek roe
1 apple
1 bunch mint

Place the flour in a bowl and gradually add the beer, whisking to avoid lumps – it should be dropping consistency. You may not need all of the beer but that is the bonus for the chef!

Lightly flour the roe. Coat well in the batter and gently drop it into a fryer until golden-brown and crispy.

Serve together with diced apple and fresh mint leaves.

Serves 4

Hot Smoked Kabeljou, Buffalo Milk Labneh
& Organic Vegetable Crudités

I remember days at Struisbaai, coming back from sea after we'd caught a few elf or katonkel. Louis, my father-in-law, would take the fish straight from the cleaning table to the garage, lightly salt them for 20 minutes, then smoke them. Maybe 2 hours after the fish was brought wriggling onto the boat, we were eating it hot smoked with some fresh bread. A great deal happens when you smoke fish, but these are a few key points.
You salt the fish to remove the moisture (10–15% weight loss of moisture from the flesh will result in a more dense, rich, enjoyable eating experience).
The heat should come from the smoke, not from the thing that is igniting the sawdust. And the heat should be gently hot, making the cooking process gradual.
Once you have hot smoked fish, let it cool slightly and then eat it before it cools completely. As the fish smokes, it releases the fat and oils in the flesh – if you refrigerate the fish, those fats set and are gone.

Smoking the Fish

50 g coarse salt
10 g brown sugar
400 g fillet of farmed kabeljou
100 g smoking chips from
   applewood or wine barrel

Mix the coarse salt and sugar and sprinkle generously over the fish fillet. Leave this for 15–20 minutes, then wash off and dry the fish.

Sprinkle the wood chips onto the bottom of the smoker. Place the fish on the rack, close the lid and gently heat until the wood chips smoke.

Depending on the amount of heat, it may take 5–10 minutes for your fish to cook and to develop a nice golden colour.

Citrus Labneh

150 ml buffalo-milk yoghurt
zest of 1 orange and 1 lemon

Labneh is a very rich, creamy, yoghurt cheese! With this dish it is a refreshing addition, especially with the added zest. To make it, just wrap a good quality yoghurt in cheesecloth and leave to hang for at least 24 hours. We use buffalo-milk yoghurt, which is very thick and creamy but is very low in lactose.

Vegetable Crudités

1 bunch baby carrots
1 fennel bulb
1 baby golden beet
1 baby purple beet
1 baby candy-stripe beet
fresh herbs for garnish

Orange Dressing

3 oranges
3 cardamom pods
1 vanilla pod
2 star anise
10 ml water
30 ml olive oil

Slice the baby vegetables as thinly as possible –
use a peeler to peel them into thin strips.

Plunge them into iced water to crisp up.

When you are about to serve your salad, drain them,
use a salad spinner if you have one to remove all of
the moisture.

Dress them with the orange dressing and fresh herbs.
Garnish with a few dried citrus segments to add a
little acidity.

Peel and segment 2 oranges, place the segments on
a non-stick tray and dry in a warm oven for 30–40
minutes.

Squeeze the juice from the remaining orange and place
in a small pot with the cardamom, vanilla and star anise;
reduce by half. Leave this to cool, then incorporate the
water and olive oil to make the dressing.

Serves 4

Oat-crusted Trout, Porcini Velouté & Pickled Wild Mushrooms

Coating a freshly caught trout in oats is very Scottish. I can remember when I was about 10 or 12 fishing with my Uncle Jimmy late at night in a loch just up from his house in the north-west of Scotland. He lives about 40 kilometres from the nearest town, so it is a very remote area. I caught a nice brown trout (he caught a few), and afterwards at home he coated the trout in oats and fried it in butter. That was our midnight snack and one that I can still taste. We didn't eat the trout with wild mushroom that evening, but Scotland is full of them. When the mushrooms start in Stellenbosch, I put this dish on the menu as it's such a delicious combination.

Oat-crusted Trout

500 g trout fillet
100 g crushed oats
1 egg white
salt and pepper to taste

Portion the trout fillet into 4 equal portions. Season the oats with salt and pepper. Brush the fillets in a little egg white then coat in the oats. Pan-fry the trout fillets in a little butter until golden brown on each side.

Porcini Velouté

100 g dried porcini
   mushrooms
olive oil
2 shallots, chopped
1 clove garlic, crushed
100 ml white wine
200 ml cream
salt and pepper to taste

Fortunately porcini are widely available in South Africa. They are quite expensive to buy in a shop, but very easy to pick while walking in a forest. You need to know where to look, but the best way to find the spots is to walk. If you cannot get fresh porcini, then dried is not a bad alternative. This recipe is made from dry porcini – if you use fresh, then reduce the amount by half. With dry porcini, first soak them in a little water to reconstitute.

Heat a pot with a little olive oil and gently sauté the shallots and garlic. Cook until translucent.

Squeeze off the reconstituted mushroom, retaining the liquid, and add this to the pot. Sauté for 1 or 2 minutes, then deglaze with the white wine.

Reduce this by half and then add the mushroom liquid and reduce by half again. If you are using fresh mushrooms, then you will need to add 200 ml fish stock here.

Once this is reduced, add the cream and cook out gently until a nice saucy consistency.

Season with salt and pepper.

Pickled Wild Mushrooms

1 part sugar
2 parts vinegar
2 parts water
200 g wild mushrooms
olive oil
chives
parsley

When making this recipe, it is a good idea to make more than you need. Pickled mushrooms are always great in a salad, and can be served with meat and fish.

When mushrooms are in season they are normally abundant, so we pick as many as we can and try to preserve them for the summer. They are so easy to pickle and this adds an extra dimension to a dish.
We pickle with a combination of water, vinegar and sugar. The degrees of the combination depend on what you are trying to pickle. You may need more vinegar for meat as it will need the acid to penetrate the heavy protein; for mushrooms the pickle is quite light.

Bring the brine (sugar, vinegar and water) to the boil.

Pour it over your clean, whole mushrooms. Cover and allow to cool.

Store in an airtight jar.

Trim the pickled mushroom, dress with olive oil and some freshly chopped herbs, such as chives or parsley.

Serves 4

Minute-cured Yellowtail, Soy & Rice Wine Dressing, Fried Zucchini & Sesame

In summer when the yellowtail run, there is an abundance of fish. Boats come into Struisbaai full, and thankfully this is when we have lots of customers who come to the restaurant to eat this dish. Yellowtail is quite an oily fish with a great firm texture similar to tuna. It is great when cooked, but excellent eaten raw or cured slightly like in this dish.

Soy Dressing

100 ml soy sauce
100 ml rice wine vinegar
100 ml water
100 g bonito flakes

Place the soy, rice wine vinegar and water into a pot. Add a large handful of the dry bonito flakes (this adds a great flavour). Bring this almost to the boil and then strain off and chill.

The dressing is all about 'sweet, sour and salty' – so taste it continuously to make sure you have a balance that suits your pallet.

1 side of yellowtail

Remove the skin and blood from the Yellowtail fillet. Cut in 1-cm thick slices like you would for sashimi (we usually serve 6 slices per person).

Place the required amount of fish in a bowl, cover with the dressing and leave for 5 minutes.

Zucchini Flowers

10 zucchini flowers
100 ml tempura batter
30 g toasted sesame seeds

Cut the flowers in half and remove the stamens.

Mix some tempura batter – we make our own but it is readily available in supermarkets.

Dip and fry the flowers for a crunchy garnish and scatter with sesame seeds.

After 5 minutes serve the fish on a plate with lots of the dressing. Place the flowers on top.

Serves 10

Hot Smoked Hake, Curly Kale
& Pine Ring Mushrooms

250 g hake

There are various methods to smoke, each with a different outcome. The temperature is key – in this recipe you want to flavour the fish without cooking it.

Lightly salt the hake for 10 minutes and then wash off.

We use apple-wood chips for smoking fish, heating them in a smoker and placing the fish in until it is smoked to our liking.

100 g kale
100 g pine ring mushrooms
100 g butter
50 g cake flour
2 cloves garlic, chopped
150 ml fish stock
20 g basil, chopped
20 g parsley, chopped
1 lemon
salt and pepper to taste

Preheat the oven to 180°C.

Wash and chop the kale ready for cooking and slice the mushrooms.

Heat 50 g of butter in a non-stick pan until foaming and turning golden-brown.

Lightly flour the fish and place into the butter. Add the mushrooms and garlic and sprinkle over the kale. Place this in the oven for 3 minutes.

Remove the fish from the pan and add the fish stock. Cook this down until it has thickened and becomes glossy. Add the chopped herbs, a squeeze of lemon juice and salt and pepper to taste.

Serves 2

Shellfish

Dealing with Wild Peacock, the pick of restaurant provisioners in the Western Cape, serves as a perfect example of why relationships with suppliers are so important. I first met Sue Baker in 1997 when I arrived at The Cellars-Hohenort Hotel from London.

The Cellars was my first position as Executive Chef, and it was to prove a great learning curve for me. Many of the suppliers I use today at Jordan were people I met through The Cellars and who helped me find my feet as a chef in a new country.

I was introduced to Sue in the hotel car park. Fredrik Aspegren, the general manager, took me over to a smiling lady standing next to a *bakkie* full of oysters.

"The Oyster Lady," he said.

And so began a long and happy relationship. We both share a passion for fine products. In the early days, when a great deal of people did not care about great produce, Sue made the effort to find the best oysters available in South Africa, then came the mussels, the quails, rabbits and other products sourced by Sue. Now the list of produce Wild Peacock offers is comprehensive. The passion she has for fine products has been passed on to Ross and Sara, who now run Wild Peacock with Sue's eye on them. Following in their mother's footsteps, new products are becoming increasingly available to chefs. Black marron, Valrhona chocolate, fine cheeses and sustainably farmed fish are all products we buy from Wild Peacock and used in this book.

The Bakers are now very close family friends of ours, even Andy Baker, who I have spent a few late nights with, shares the passion for sourcing great products and making Wild Peacock the producer most chefs in the region would count as their favourite.

Freshwater Crayfish, Young Beets, Fennel Crudités, Aioli & Orange Water Dressing

Crayfish

4 crayfish
salt and pepper to taste

Boil the crayfish in salted water for 4 minutes, then chill in iced water. Peel the crayfish, pick all of the meat out of the claws and chill.

To serve, dress the crayfish with the orange dressing and season with salt and pepper.

Aioli

2 eggs
2 cloves garlic
200 ml extra virgin olive oil

Blend the eggs and garlic until smooth, then gradually add 100 ml olive oil and season with salt and pepper.

Labneh

50 g buffalo-milk yoghurt
1 lemon
1 orange

Hang the yoghurt in cheesecloth overnight to remove any excess moisture. If you cannot find buffalo-milk yoghurt then use a good quality, minimally processed yoghurt.

Mix in the zest of 1 lemon and orange to flavour.

Orange Dressing

3 oranges
juice of 1 lemon
25 ml water
50 ml olive oil

Zest, peel and segment the oranges, place the juice from the oranges and lemon in a pot and reduce with a gradual heat by half. Strain the reduced liquid and measure 50 ml, place this in a blender with a pinch of the zest and emulsify with 25 ml water and 50 ml olive oil.

Lay the segments onto a non-stick tray and dry in an oven at 60°C for 2 hours.

Beetroot

250 g baby beetroot

Wash and then wrap the beets in tin foil and bake at 180°C for 30 minutes or until cooked.

Peel while warm and reserve until needed.

Fennel

1 large fennel bulb with leaves

Pick off the nice fennel leaves to use as a garnish, then slice the fennel thinly. You can even use a peeler for this. Dress this with a little lemon juice and olive oil.

Garnish

25 g chives, chopped
25 g flat-leaf parsley, chopped

Garnish with the fresh herbs.

Serves 4

Saldanha Bay Oysters, Rhubarb & Chorizo Crumble

Saldanha Bay oysters from the cold Atlantic are delicious natural but this dressing adds even more depth of flavour.

Rhubarb and Chorizo Crumble

25 g butter
50 g ciabatta crumbs
15 g grated Parmesan

Heat the butter in a non-stick pan until golden and foaming and add the crumbs, stirring continuously until golden brown and crunchy.

At this point add the Parmesan and cook for a further 30 seconds.

Spread this on kitchen roll to remove any excess butter.

---

100 g rhubarb
50 g spicy chorizo sausage
100 ml olive oil
salt and pepper to taste
20 g chopped chives

Peel and dice the rhubarb into small blocks. Cut the chorizo a little larger.

In a non-stick pan, gently fry the chorizo with a little olive oil. Once it begins to colour, add the rhubarb and cook out for 1 or 2 minutes. Add the remainder of the olive oil.

The rhubarb must be soft but not disintegrated.

Season this with a little salt and pepper and add the chopped chives.

---

6 oysters

Shuck the oysters, spoon a generous amount of the rhubarb dressing onto the oyster and cover with the crumbs.

Serves 2–6

Wild Oysters from Vleesbaai,
Spicy Sago & Seaweed

Wild oysters are flatter than rock oysters and have a lovely nutty flavour. You can use a rock oyster as an alternative.

Sago

50 g sago
1 litre water

Bring the water to the boil in a sauce pan.

Add the sago, whisking to make sure it separates. Leave to cook for 3–5 minutes. The sago will become translucent with just a speck of white in the centre.

At this point, strain into a sieve and run cold water over it to stop cooking. Drain off any excess water and mix with a touch of olive oil to keep separate.

Spicy Dressing

10 g chopped chilli
10 g crushed garlic
juice of 2 limes
20 ml soy sauce
fish sauce to taste

Crush the garlic and chilli with a pestle to a fine paste.

Add the soy and lime and then gradually add the fish sauce to taste. You are looking for a balance between sour and salty.

6 oysters

To serve, shuck the oysters, removing any broken pieces of shell. Place a little of the sago in a bowl and moisten with the dressing. Spoon this over the oyster. We garnish these oysters with a little seaweed.

Serves 2–6

Crayfish with Smoked Tomato Risotto

Smoked Tomato

1 kg vine-ripened tomato

Blanch and peel the tomatoes, cut into quarters and dry off any excess moisture. Keep the peeling and trimmings for the stock. Dry the tomato gently in a warm oven until slightly dehydrated.

Smoke the tomatoes in a smoker but do not discolour the tomato as you want the flavour to be intense but not overpower the risotto.

Crayfish

4 crayfish
1 carrot
1 head celery
1 bunch leeks
5 g tomato paste
1 bulb garlic

Boil the crayfish for 4 minutes, then refresh in ice water. Separate the legs, tails and body. We use the meat inside the legs for the risotto base, the tails roasted and the bodies for the stock and garnish.

For the stock, roast the shells in a pot with 50 g butter. Add the chopped carrot, celery, leek, tomato paste and 2 cloves of garlic and cover with water.

Simmer for 1 hour, then strain.

Clean the tails and refrigerate until needed.

Pick all the meat from the legs and chop up.

Risotto

250 g Arborio rice
1 lemon
1 bulb garlic
6 shallots finely chopped
250 g butter
25 g basil
100 g Parmesan

Add olive oil to a heavy-based pot and sweat off the shallots. Keep stirring as you do not want any colour.

Once translucent, add the chopped crayfish legs and the rice and cook for 4 minutes, stirring.

Gradually add the crayfish stock, stirring occasionally. The rice should absorb the stock. Add the smoked tomato to taste and the remainder of the stock. The rice should be cooked after 10–12 minutes. Test a kernel to see if it is cooked – we prefer our rice to be slightly al dente.
Once the rice is cooked, slowly incorporate the remainder of the butter, the basil and finally the Parmesan. Leave to rest for 2–3 minutes.

The risotto should be creamy and rich. If it is too dry, add a little stock or water to achieve the desired consistency.

Roast the crayfish tails in foaming butter with salt and pepper until golden.

Serves 4

Mussel Papillotte, Coconut Milk, Chilli, Ginger & Garlic

We get fantastic mussels from Saldanha Bay. The mussels need to be cleaned before cooking. They have beards which they use to attach themselves to rocks so make sure you pull all of these out.

250 g black mussels
1 lime, quartered
1 chilli, chopped
1 bulb garlic, crushed
100 ml coconut milk
1 stick of lemongrass, bruised
1 bunch coriander, chopped
10 g flat-leaf parsley, chopped

Place the washed mussels into a large pot with all other ingredients, except coriander and parsley.

Place the lid on the pot and boil until the mussels are opened. This should take no more than 5 minutes.

Roughly chop the coriander and parsley and add before eating.

To serve 'en papillotte', line a bowl with a large square of baking paper (40 cm²), with a smaller square of tin foil (15 cm²) at the centre. Scoop cooked mussels and a generous helping of sauce and roll to create a bag. Open at the table to release some steam and a wonderful aroma.

Alternatively, serve in a deep bowl with fresh bread.

1 portion

Fruit

Growing your own veggies or picking fruit from a tree in your garden is a rewarding part of being a chef. It's like you follow a certain ingredient on the whole journey from seed to table.

There's a whole lot of chatter in the industry about farm-to-fork food and so on. I don't really worry about all that, I just enjoy going and getting my lettuce or some beans out of the garden.

Around June, regulars at Jordan start to notice quite a bit of guava appearing on the menu. There's a great big guava tree at home, and the boys and I pick almost every day in season. The fruit gets processed into jams, jellies, ice cream and all sorts of other things. It's a very versatile fruit, and being a Scot, if it comes off a tree for free, it's all right with me.

We also keep a veggie patch at Jordan where we grow Jerusalem artichokes, broad beans, peas, kale and globe artichokes. Every year Gary Jordan and I walk around, looking at the space and discussing what did well last year and where we will plant it for the next season.

Shortening the journey from picking to kitchen and doing it in season really allows you to capture the flavour of an ingredient in a dish. But it's also just a nice thing to do to wander around the garden when you arrive at work in the morning.

A lot of inspiration for dishes comes from my little visits to pick herbs or check on the kale. I wonder if that would go with this, or if a purée of something might do well with a particular tomato that's ripening. Gary is great at sourcing interesting stuff for us to grow, particularly heirloom tomatoes.

Caramelised Fig Tart, Gorgonzola, Hazelnut & Watercress

Fortunately the Cape is full of fig trees and around the end of December we start to get the new season's crop. We get many varieties of fig – each has differences that make figs a very versatile ingredient to use in the restaurant. We serve small eve figs with duck or game, green Cape figs poached, we make preserve for our cheese room from the unripe Cape fig but the large juicy black mission fig is great for this tart.

We have a cheese room at the restaurant and sell a great local gorgonzola from Cremalat, which is probably the most popular cheese in the room. We crumble some onto the tart and make a Chantilly to add a different dimension.

Caramelised Fig Tart

100 g castor sugar
100 g butter
250 g butter puff pastry
16 ripe figs

Caramelise the sugar and butter. The caramel needs to be quite dark but not burnt, the bitterness of the caramel works well with the sweet figs and even better with the gorgonzola.

Once you have a caramel, cover the bases of your 10-cm tart moulds with a thin layer and leave to set.

Wash the figs, cut into halves and arrange onto the caramel. Leave a little gap at the edge for the pastry to touch the caramel.

Cut your puff pastry slightly bigger that the rim of the tart mould and place on top. Use the back of a spoon to push the pastry in at the edges.

Bake the tarts at 180°C for around 15 minutes until golden brown; the caramel should be bubbling around the edges.

Gorgonzola Chantilly

50 ml thick cream
50 g gorgonzola
50 ml whipped cream
salt and pepper to taste

Heat the thick cream and melt the gorgonzola in it.

Place this melted creamy mix on an ice bath to cool.

It will begin to thicken as it cools. This is when you fold in the whipped cream, season and chill until needed.

Hazelnut Dressing

5 ml sherry vinegar
20 ml olive oil
10 ml hazelnut oil
10 g roasted hazelnuts, crushed
salt and pepper to taste

Combine the vinegar and oils, then add the nuts and season.

Makes 4 tarts

Caramelised Banana Tart, Butterscotch & Prune Ice Cream

Caramelised Banana Tart

100 g castor sugar
100 g butter
100 ml cream
3 bananas
250 g butter puff pastry

Heat the sugar with the butter and caramelise until golden brown.

Once you have a caramel, cover the bases of your 10-cm tart moulds with a thin layer and leave to set.

Use the remainder of the caramel to make the butterscotch sauce – simply add cream to the caramel and boil.

Peel and slice the banana and arrange onto the caramel. Leave a little gap at the edge for the pastry to touch the caramel.

Cut your puff pastry slightly bigger that the rim of the tart mould and place on top. Use the back of a spoon to push the pastry in at the edges.

Bake the tarts at 180°C for around 15 minutes until golden brown; the caramel should be bubbling around the edges.

Pour the butterscotch onto a plate for presentation.

Remove your tarts from the moulds before the sugar sets.

We garnish our tarts with banana paper, which is pureed banana spread out on greaseproof paper and dehydrated.

Prune Ice Cream

300 ml milk
300 ml cream
50 g prunes soaked in rum
6 egg yolks
200 g sugar

Slowly bring the milk and cream up to just below the boil.

Cut the prunes into rough pieces and add to the milk to soak.

In a bowl, combine the egg and sugar until well incorporated.

Combine all the ingredients and cook gently until it begins to thicken, chill this immediately, then churn in an ice cream machine until done.

If you do not have an ice cream machine, buy a good quality ice cream from your local deli.

Makes 6 tarts

Coconut Panna Cotta, Aromatic Sago & Cardamom Ice Cream

Panna Cotta

500 ml coconut milk
100 ml milk
castor sugar
gelatin leaves

Heat the coconut milk and the milk, sweeten to your liking with sugar.

Soak the gelatin leaves in ice water and add to the warmed milk, make sure the gelatin is dissolved, then chill.

Before it sets, pour it into your serving dishes and refrigerate.

Sago

50 g sago
100 ml coconut milk
1 vanilla pod
2 cardamom pods
2 star anise
1 stick lemongrass

Fill a sauce pan with water and bring to the boil, add the sago and whisk to avoid lumps.
Cook this until just the centre is white, then strain off and chill immediately.

Heat the coconut milk with the aromatics and infuse. Sweeten with a little sugar if necessary.

To serve, mix the sago with the coconut milk.

Cardamom Ice Cream

300 ml milk
300 ml cream
25 g cardamom pods
6 egg yolks
250 g sugar

Slowly bring the milk and cream up to just below the boil and add the cardamom.

In a bowl, combine the egg yolks and sugar until well incorporated.

Combine all the ingredients and cook gently until it begins to thicken.

Chill this immediately, then churn in an ice cream machine until done.

If you do not have an ice cream machine, buy a good quality ice cream from your local deli.

Serves 6

Compressed Spanspek Melon, Lime Jelly, Melon Sorbet & Mint

Here is another very refreshing dessert, great for a hot summer lunch. From mid-summer for a few weeks we get fresh spanspek from the farm down the road. They are so juicy and refreshing it is difficult not to eat them all fresh. We compress the melon in a vacuum machine. This changes the texture, firming up the melon and intensifying the flavour. You could just slice fresh melon for a great result.

Compressed Spanspek Melon

1 spanspek melon
mint leaves for garnish

Cut the melon into quarters and remove the skin and seeds. Blend one of the quarters for the sorbet and place the others in a vacuum bag and vacuum on a high setting to compress.

Keep this chilled until needed. Just before you plate your dessert you can slice the melon into thin strips to arrange on the plate.

Lime Jelly

3 gelatin leaves
50 ml water
25 g sugar
100 ml lime juice
5 g lime zest

Sponge the gelatin in iced water until soft.

Heat the water and sugar, then add the gelatin.
Once the gelatin has dissolved, add the lime juice and chill on a tray.

This will be cut into cubes to add a sour flavour to the sweet melon.

Bring a little water to the boil in a small pot, add the zest and boil for 20 seconds. Strain this off, then repeat two more times. This will remove the bitter oils from the zest.

Once you have done this three times, toss the zest in a little castor sugar and keep to garnish your melon.

Melon Sorbet

180 ml water
30 g glucose
50 g sugar
65 g melon purée
juice of 1 lemon

Bring the water, glucose and sugar to the boil, then remove from the heat and add the fruit purée, strain this and chill.

Once cool, add the lemon juice for acidity and churn in an ice cream machine or freeze in a shallow tray and blend once frozen.

Serves 4

Poached Dalsig Guava, Guava Mousse & Guava Sorbet

Fortunately we have a guava tree in our garden which fills up with fruit every year, so much that the branches droop until they almost touch the ground. I get my boys to pick them, for a small price of course, and use them in the restaurant and the bakery.

Guava has an intoxicating floral aroma that perfumes the whole house once they have been picked, but the flavour is quite subtle. This dessert is very light and refreshing and is very popular at the restaurant.

Poaching Guavas

250 ml Noble Late Harvest
    dessert wine
250 ml water
150 g sugar
5 cardamom pods
3 star anise
2 vanilla pods
rind of 1 orange
1 kg guavas

Place all ingredients into a large pot and slowly bring to the boil.

Peel the guavas and place into the pot and slowly poach until soft but not mushy. You need to maintain some of the texture of the fruit.

Once cooked, which will take around 15 minutes, leave to cool in the poaching liquid. To prepare the guavas, remove from the syrup and cut into quarters, remove the seeds from the flesh, keep this aside for the sorbet and place the flesh quarters back into the syrup.
This can now be refrigerated for a few days if required.

Place all of the trimmings from the guavas into a blender and make into a smooth paste. We will use this paste to flavour the mousse and the sorbet.

Guava Sorbet

180 ml water
50 g sugar
30 g glucose
65 g guava puree
juice of 1 lemon

Bring the water, glucose and sugar to the boil, then remove from the heat and add the fruit purée, strain and chill.

Once cool, add the lemon juice for acidity and churn in an ice cream machine or freeze in a shallow tray and blend once frozen.

Guava Mousse

3 egg yolks
60 g castor sugar
100 ml milk
3 gelatin leaves
100 g guava purée
150 g whipped cream

Combine the egg yolks and sugar with a whisk.

Bring the milk to the boil and pour over the egg and sugar. Mix this immediately as it will begin to cook the egg. Return to the pot and gently cook on a low heat for 2 minutes.

Sponge the gelatin in iced water and add with the purée to the custard. Cool this down until it begins to set. Then fold in the whipped cream and place into a piping bag.

Brandy Snap

25 g butter
25 g sugar
25 g honey
25 g flour

Melt the butter, sugar and honey, then fold in the flour.

Make this into balls and bake on non-stick paper until golden brown. The mix will spread out in the oven.

As soon as it is cooked, we roll the brandy snap around a wooden spoon handle to create the cylinder.

Once cylinders are cooled, you can pipe the mousse into them. This adds a nice crunchy texture to the dish.

Serve the poached guavas covered with the syrup and garnish with some rosemary and lavender flowers.

Serves 6

Riesling-poached Cape Fig, Frozen Yoghurt & Pistachio Brittle

Riesling Poached Cape Figs

500 ml Riesling
200 g sugar
3 star anise
3 cardamom pods
1 vanilla pod
1 orange
12 figs
1 spring rose geranium

Heat the Riesling with the sugar, star anise, cardamom and vanilla.

Peel the orange and add the peel to the warm Riesling.

Cross the tops of the figs across the stems and place into the Riesling. Poach until cooked.

Remove from the heat, add the rose geranium and chill until needed.

Frozen Yoghurt

200 ml milk
1 vanilla pod
6 egg yolks
125 g sugar
300 g buffalo-milk yoghurt

You can buy good quality frozen yoghurt, but if you feel like a light challenge and have an ice cream machine, try your own. We use buffalo-milk yoghurt for our recipe because it has a higher cream content and adds a great richness and dimension to the finished product.

Heat the milk and vanilla.

Mix the yolk of the eggs with the sugar and incorporate into the milk. Cook this for 2 minutes on a very low heat to form a custard.

Add the yoghurt to the custard and chill.

Freeze in an ice cream machine.

Pistachio Brittle

30 g pistachio nuts
150 g castor sugar
4 g bicarbonate soda
10 g butter

Roast the pistachio nuts in a hot oven for 2–3 minutes, then crush and reserve.

Caramelise the sugar slowly until golden brown. Add the pistachio, the bicarb and the butter and mix quickly.

Pour onto greaseproof paper and spread out. Break off shards of this and crumble over the figs when you serve.

Serves 4

Fowl

In my kitchen, there is a lot of emphasis on technique. The produce, ingredients, relationships with suppliers and customers are all very well, but if you don't have the first clue how to carve a roast or dress a carcass, you're nowhere. It's something we are always looking at, and it means we're passing the skills on to the younger cooks.

Technique begins with simple stuff like making stocks or pastries and so forth. But there's a whole lot more to being a cook, with things like de-boning a chicken or duck. I think a lot of the old skills of cooking are being lost in restaurant kitchens that focus on producing a set list of things in a certain way. It's all very well getting dishes onto the pass as quickly as possible and doing the numbers in the restaurant, but doing so sacrifices some of what it means to be a cook.

There are suppliers who will deliver de-boned birds or ready-butchered venison. But we avoid that at Jordan. I like to deal with the whole animal. That way, you have the bones and off-cuts left for stocks and soups. It's also an opportunity to teach members of the crew new skills, or keep their hands busy. Part of the joy of cooking is in the doing, and if you're doing the same thing over and over, you might as well be assembling cars.

Something like a chicken balontine may seem like a hell of a lot of work for what amounts to a chicken dish, but the skill is the point here. The technique calls on a whole range of skills, from knife-work and boning, to mincing and tying-off with string that I love to see in use in the kitchen.

Balontine of Chicken, Wild Mushroom Farce, Roasted Pine Rings & Rosemary Jus

Every year, starting with the first rains at the end of May, the forest begins to wake up. First the herbs start to grow so we pick sorrel, chickweed and nasturtium. The first porcini start to come around this time, causing great excitement in the kitchen; if we are lucky we can pick quite a harvest.
Then when the rain really comes and the forest is soaked more into June, pine ring mushrooms appear. We pick in the morning before service or during our split shift when we have dinner. Not only is it good to cook with these ingredients, it is great fun and exercise getting out into the forest.

1 free-range chicken
1 egg
100 ml cream
250 g wild mushrooms
6 basil leaves
salt and pepper
rosemary

Starting at the back of the chicken, remove the skin and flesh from the carcass. This is a little tricky but should be manageable if you take your time. As we are stuffing and rolling the chicken, try not to break the skin.

Once you have removed the carcass, pull out both legs and trim out the wing bones. You are left with the skin of the chicken with the breast attached.

Dice up the meat from the legs and fry in a little butter.

Remove the breast from the skin and separate the little fillets from the main breast. Put the fillets into a food processor and blend until smooth. Add 1 egg white and 100 ml cream and blend until it forms a smooth mousse.

Clean and sauté the mushrooms, and then chop into a rough paste. Combine the chicken mousse with the chopped mushroom and cooked diced leg meat. This is the stuffing for the chicken.

Lay the basil leaves on the skin of the chicken, then one of the breasts onto the basil. Add a thick layer of the stuffing, then the last breast. Roll this up in the skin and tie with string.

Roast the chicken bones and make a stock that you can reduce with the rosemary for the sauce.

To cook the balontine, gently brown the chicken in some butter, then wrap it in tin foil and bake at 180°C for 20 minutes. Once cooked, allow a resting period of 5 minutes before slicing.

Serves 5

Stuffed Quail, Basil & Aubergine, Aubergine Velouté & Crispy Sage

This may look like a great deal of effort for such a small bird, but the combination is delicious and it is easier to eat a deboned quail. It may even seem like too much trouble to debone a quail, if so, then roast the quail whole and use the stuffing as a garnish. It is possible to re-create this dish at home. I recently presented a cooking class for one of our regular guests who requested this dish. Seven out of 8 quails looked pretty good, one looked like a starved sparrow.

Stuffing

1 large aubergine
salt and pepper
olive oil
1 bunch basil
4 cloves garlic
3 anchovies
10 g Dijon mustard
30 g crème fraîche
1 lime

Peel the aubergine and cut into 8–12 segments, depending on the size of aubergine. Season this with salt, pepper and olive oil and place on a sheet of tin foil.

Remove the leaves from the basil and reserve, but keep the stalks and place on top of the aubergine.

Cut the garlic cloves in half with the skin on and place both halves directly onto the foil. We want the garlic to caramelise.

Place another piece of foil onto this, seal the edges and bake at 200°C for 20–30 minutes until the aubergine is very soft.

Once the aubergine is soft, remove 2 of the nicest strips – we will use this for the stuffing. Place the remainder into a blender with the garlic, anchovies, mustard and crème fraîche and blend until smooth.

Season with salt, pepper and a little lime juice, then chill until needed.

Quail

1 quail
50 g net fat
olive oil
butter
250 ml hot chicken stock

We want to remove the bone from the quail, retaining as much skin intact as possible. Start from the breastbone and work the knife along the bone of the carcass to remove the meat from the quail.

You should or could end up with two halves of the quail, boneless apart from the leg and wing.

Cut the wing at the middle joint and clean off the meat to make a nice garnish. Remove the thighbone, leaving the drumstick attached.

You should now have a half quail, boneless apart from the wing bone clean and the drumstick.

Lay this out skin-side down and season with salt and pepper. Place 3 basil leaves covering the breast, then a strip of aubergine. Roll this up into a sausage shape with a bone sticking out at each end.

Lay out a square of net fat and roll the quail in this. This will help to secure the quail as we cook it.

To cook the quail, gently heat a non-stick pan and add a little olive oil and a knob of butter. Just as the butter starts to foam and turn golden, add the quail and gently seal on all sides, then place in a pre-heated oven for 3–4 minutes at 180°C.

Once cooked, remove and allow to rest for 5 minutes before slicing.

Crispy Sage

sage
50 g butter

Sage has a great savoury flavour and can be used for chicken, duck, fish and of course quail. Heat 50 g butter in a non-stick pan until it foams, add the sage and cook until it is crispy.

Serves 2

'Duck Toast', Quince Jam, Confit Gizzards, Rillettes, Parfait & Celeriac Chantilly

We buy whole ducks at the restaurant and like to utilise the whole animal – nothing goes to waste.

Brioche

1 kg cake flour
90 g castor sugar
20 g fine salt
30 g instant yeast
11 eggs
300 g butter

Brioche is relatively easy and good fun to make. If you do not have time, it is available to buy at Jordan Bakery daily.

Combine all dry ingredients in a mixer and then slowly incorporate the eggs.

When the eggs are fully incorporated, gradually add the butter.

Knead this into a ball and prove in a warm place for 2–3 hours.

After 2–3 hours the dough should have doubled in size, knock this back and shape into the loaf tin. Leave to prove again until it has doubled in size. Brush the proofed loaf with egg yolk and bake at 180°C for 45 minutes.

Makes 1 kg loaf tin

Rillettes

Rillettes is a rough paté of confit meat and fat. Usually it is made with pork but we make it with the duck legs.

4 duck legs
4 duck gizzards
250 g coarse salt
peel of 1 orange
5 g fennel seeds
5 g coriander seeds
5 g star anise
50 g brown sugar
1 kg duck fat

Wash the duck legs and gizzards and dry with kitchen paper. Mix all dry ingredients and cover the duck legs and gizzards to cure. After 6 hours, wash the salt mix off the legs and pat dry.

Place the cured duck legs in a small pot with the duck fat and cook at 90°C for 4–5 hours. The meat will become very soft, so be careful when handling it as it will fall off the bone.

Once the meat is cool, remove it from the pan, keeping the gizzards separate. We need the leg meat for the rillettes so remove the meat from the bone and place in a bowl. Shred the meat until fine strips, then add the duck fat and work into a wet paste. Season this with salt and pepper and refrigerate to set.

Duck Breast

1 duck breast

Clean the breast of any sinew and score the fat diagonally. Season the breast with salt and pepper and fry gently skin side down in a non-stick pan to render the fat on the breast. Keep the heat at its lowest setting.

When the fat has almost gone, turn up the heat to finish off the cooking, flip the breast onto the flesh side and cook for 1 minute. Remove from the pan and allow to rest.

Duck Liver Paté

250 g duck livers
1 large onion, sliced
3 cloves garlic, crushed
1 bunch thyme
50 ml port
250 g butter
salt and pepper to taste

Clean and trim the livers and dry on kitchen paper.

Sauté the onions and garlic until caramelised, add 3 or 4 sprigs of thyme then deglaze with the port and reduce until sticky.

Heat the butter in a pot and fry the duck livers until they are cooked. Add the onions to this and blend in a food processor until smooth. Season with the salt and pepper, strain through a fine sieve and cool.

Celeriac Chantilly

1 bulb celeriac
1 litre milk
salt and pepper
50 g butter
100 ml whipped cream

Peel and dice the celeriac, place in a pot with the milk and boil until soft. Strain off the milk and blend the celeriac with the butter; season this with salt and pepper. Once the purée is cool, weigh off 100 g and fold 100 ml whipped cream into it. Chill this until needed.

Slice the brioche and fry in a little duck fat until golden brown. Spread some quince jam onto the brioche.

Slice the duck breast as thinly as possible and arrange onto the toast.

Fry the gizzards until crispy and place these on the toast.

Arrange a few spoons of the pate and celeriac and serve with a little dressed watercress.

Makes 4–6 starters

Air-dried Duck Breast, Orange Water Dressing, Orange Purée & Fennel

Duck

50 g coarse sea salt
20 g brown sugar
1 bunch of fennel leaves
1 g coriander seeds
1 g white peppercorns
1 star anise
2 large duck breasts

Combine all the ingredients except the duck in a food processor.

Trim any excess sinew off the duck breast, place into a tray and cover with the curing mix. Place this in the fridge for 24 hours.

After 24 hours, wash the breast and pat dry. Hang the breast in a dry area for 1 week. We use a dehydrator for this, which speeds up the process. The meat will shrink and dry and after 1 week you can cut thin slices off the breast. I like it when it is still quite moist and not too dry.

Dressing and Orange Purée

4 oranges
10 g unsalted butter

Peel the oranges, segment and squeeze out all of the juice, keeping the peel and pith for the purée.

Place the peel in a pot and cover with water, bring this to a boil, then discard the water and repeat the process.

We boil the oranges 4–5 times to remove the bitter oils.

Place the cooked peel into a blender and add the unsalted butter. Blend until smooth, pass through a fine sieve and chill.

Place the orange segments on a non-stick mat in a very low oven until semi dried.

Orange Dressing

juice from 4 oranges
2 star anise
2 cardamom pods
1 vanilla pod
50 ml extra virgin olive oil
salt and pepper to taste

Reduce the juice with the star anise, cardamom and vanilla to a light syrup, then strain, chill and combine with the olive oil and a little water.

Serves 4

Twice-cooked Crispy Duck, Honeyed Parsnips & Spicy Greens

This is a method of cooking duck that I learnt while working in South East Asia. It does take some time but the results are well worth the effort. The only problem with this dish is that it is so tasty, you eat too much.

Crispy Duck

6 star anise
6 cardamom pods
20 g palm sugar
3 sticks of lemongrass
100 ml sweet Indonesian
  soy sauce
100 ml soy sauce
50 g ginger
1 bulb garlic
100 ml honey
2 oranges
1 lemon
1 fat duck

Place all ingredients, apart from the duck, oranges and lemon, into a large pot. Halve and squeeze out the oranges and lemon, add 5 litres of water and bring up to the boil.

Wash the duck and trim off the parson's nose – the bit at the back that produces the preen oils that make the duck float.

Add the duck to the boiling stock and simmer for 45 minutes. Make sure the duck is submerged. Remove the duck from the stock and hang somewhere with a good air circulation to dry. We hang ours in front of an electric fan for 12 hours, the drier you make it, the crispier the end product.

Once the duck is dry, bake in an oven at 180°C for a further 45 minutes.

When cool, remove the breast and the legs and place the bones and trimmings back into the stock. Simmer for 2–3 hours to add flavour to the stock.

You can reduce a little of this stock to a glaze for the duck and freeze the remainder for the next time. Keeping the stock and reusing it each time will make your ducks better and better.

Spicy Greens

cucumber
spring onion
kale
green beens
coriander
parsley
100 ml spicy dressing

The spicy greens add refreshment to the rich duck. We julienne all green vegetables and dress with the spicy dressing from the kale recipe (see page 168) and toasted sesame seeds.

To serve, place the duck on a tray and grill under a salamander or grill to crisp up. Brush with a little duck fat or olive oil. We serve it with the honeyed parsnip purée (see page 177).

Once you have reduced your cooking liquid, add a knob of butter to it and spoon over the duck.

Serves 2

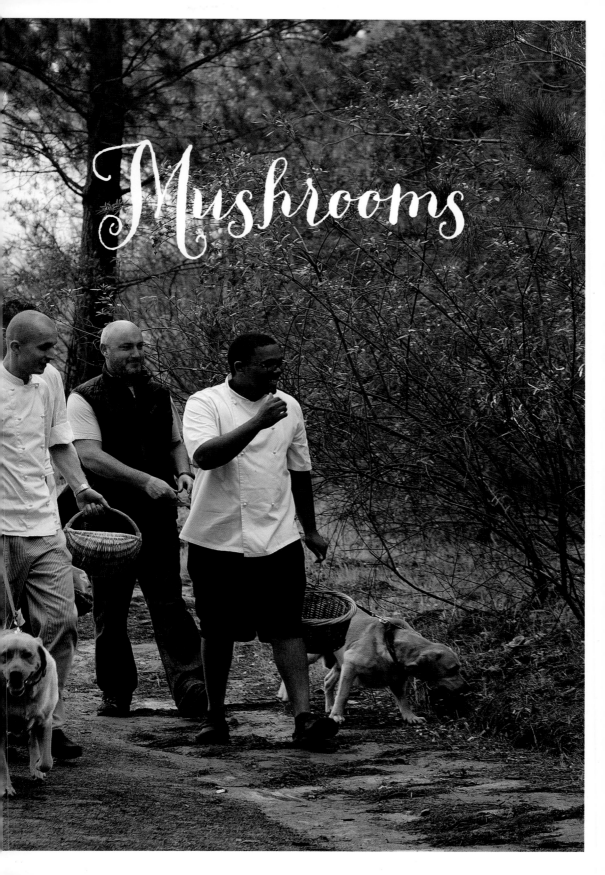

Mushrooms

Living in Stellenbosch is great. It offers so much to do and the proximity to mountains and nature is just awesome. I can mountain bike on the trails in the nearby parks and forests, run the dogs and enjoy an outdoor lifestyle.

But there's more … there's food in them hills. Foraging has become a big trend among chefs, it's like a new catch-word. There are talented young guys going for walks and collecting pine needles to make special syrups and finding wild asparagus for salads and so on and that's great. But foraging isn't new – we've been doing it in my family since I was a wee boy. My sister and I would go looking for brambles and elderberries which my grandmother would make into jam.

So imagine how happy I was when I found pine ring mushrooms growing in the forests at Paradyskloof. Wild mushrooms are always a delight on the menu. Dale and the crew always make an outing of mushrooming in season. After a couple of days of rain, we drive up early in the morning, or after lunch service, with baskets or tubs and see what we can find. There are times when there are so many on the ground we come back with bucket-loads. We then have to free one of the team to concentrate on pickling or preparing them for drying.

These outings are about team-building as they are always fun, but they're also about what we do. I like the idea that the team are getting out into the fresh air and remembering that ingredients don't just arrive in a van. It's like getting city kids to milk a cow. What we do as cooks is closely and wonderfully tied up with nature. Going for a walk in a forest and finding something to eat just reinforces that.

'Chef's Breakfast' of Roasted Marrow, Wild Mushroom & Brioche

This is a monster breakfast that we serve occasionally in the bakery. If you have a big day ahead then start with this and it will keep you going.

Marrow

4 marrow bones
1 clove of garlic
1 cup of flour for dusting
1 stick rosemary

Dust the marrow in the flour and then pan fry in oil until golden brown on each side. Roughly chop the garlic and rosemary and sprinkle on top. Roast this in a hot oven for 10–15 minutes.

2 slices toasted brioche

Toast the brioche, spoon the mushroom on top and serve with the bones. You may like a wedge of lemon to cut the richness of the dish.

Mushrooms

100 g assorted mushrooms
1 clove garlic
50 ml cream
5 g butter

Cut up the mushrooms into even-sized pieces and fry gently in a little butter. Add 1 clove of crushed garlic, the cream and butter and reduce until quite thick.

Serves 2

Terrine of Braised Springbok, Poached Kumquats & Pickled Pine Ring Mushrooms

You can't really make a small terrine so this is a starter to prepare for 8–10 guests. It is, however, worth the effort and something that can be done a day or two in advance.

Braised Springbok

1 springbok shoulder
  on the bone
50 g carrots
50 g leeks
50 g large onion
50 g celery
1 bulb garlic
1 bay leaf
1 bottle red wine
2 litre chicken stock
250 g pine ring mushrooms
10 g parsley, chopped

Season and brown the springbok shoulder in a little oil.

Roughly chop the vegetables and roast them in the same pan.

Place the springbok into a large pot and add the vegetables and bay leaf. Deglaze the pan with the red wine and reduce until half.

Add the chicken stock and bring up to the boil, then slowly braise the meat in the oven for 4–5 hours at 120°C until soft and tender.

Clean the pine ring mushrooms and cut in half, then gently fry in olive oil until cooked. Chill these until ready to assemble.

To assemble the terrine, drain off the stock and reduce to 1 litre. This should contain enough gelatin to set the terrine.

Break the meat into golf ball-sized chunks and place in a bowl. Season well with salt and pepper, add the mushrooms and the chopped parsley, then pour over the cooking liquid.

Place all of this into your 2-litre terrine mould and press with a light weight. Chill for 24 hours.

Poached kumquats

150 g kumquats

The kumquats add a great sweet and sour flavour to the dish and go very well with springbok.

To prepare them we first have to remove the bitter oils from the skin. Boil water in a pot and add the kumquats. When it comes back up to the boil, drain off the liquid and repeat this process 3–4 times.

Then make syrup with equal sugar and water and bring to the boil. Poach the kumquats in this for 5–10 minutes.

Serves 8–10

Autumnal Salad, Jerusalem Artichoke, Onion Chantilly & Wild Herbs

When the pine ring mushrooms come, they come! The forests are full of them and we take every opportunity to pick them and use them in the restaurant. This is an excellent salad starter for the autumn and winter months.

Jerusalem Artichokes

250 g Jerusalem artichokes
150 ml cream
1 garlic clove

We prepare the artichokes a couple of ways for this dish.

Wash and slice 200 g and fry in a little butter until caramelised. This will take at least 1 hour and should not be rushed. Once they are soft and caramelised, add 100 ml of cream and blend into a smooth paste.

Wash the remainder of the artichokes. Slice half of them to be deep fried into crisps. Bake the other half in the oven until soft to use in the salad.

Pickled Pine Ring Mushrooms

300 ml water
100 ml white wine vinegar
10 g salt
2 bay leaves
250 g pine ring mushrooms

Combine all ingredients except the mushrooms and bring to the boil, then remove from the heat.

Clean the mushrooms and pour the brine over them.

Leave this for at least 1 day before using the mushrooms.

Onion Chantilly

1 large onion
salt and pepper

Wrap the onion in tin foil and bake at 120°C for 8 hours.

Once cooked, remove the foil and skin from the onion and blend into a smooth paste. Whip the remainder of the cream and fold into the onion purée, season with salt and pepper. Spoon some chantilly to add some complexity to the mushroom.

When serving the dish, sauté half of the mushrooms to add a contrast in flavour and texture.

We serve this dish with herbs which we pick in the forest. Nasturtiums add a great flavour, woodsorrel has a sour flavour and chickweed has a very earthy flavour. Each one compliments the flavour of the artichokes and mushrooms.

Serves 4

Pan-roasted Kabeljou, Winter Vegetables & Wild Mushroom Bouillon

Kabeljou

300 g kabeljou fillet
salt and pepper to taste

Ask the fishmonger to trim the fish and cut into two nice portions, keeping any trimmings or bones to make the fish stock.

When required, season the skin side with fine salt and pepper and pan fry on the skin in olive oil until crispy and golden brown.

Flip it over for 30 seconds to finish cooking.

Bouillon and Wild Mushroom Duexelles

6 sliced shallots
2 clove garlic crushed
1 glass white wine
250 ml fish stock
10 g dried porcini
assorted winter vegetables
50 g mixed wild mushroom
50 g crème fraîche
1 stick tarragon

Sauté half of the shallots and half of the garlic in a large pot, then deglaze with the white wine and reduce by half. Add the fish stock, the dry porcini and tarragon and simmer gently. Poach your vegetables in this bouillon to maximise the flavour.

Sauté the remainder of the shallots and garlic in a frying pan, finely chop the wild mushroom and add.

Cook this out until dry, then season with salt and pepper and chill. Once cool, fold in the crème fraîche.

Serves 2

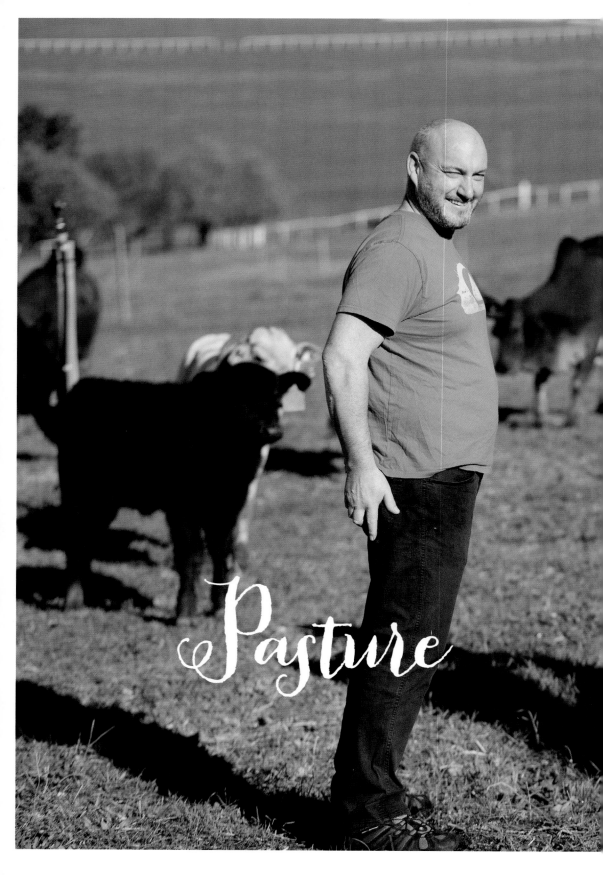

Pasture

One of the suppliers I really enjoy dealing with is Ryan Boon. Ryan is a butcher who really knows his craft. He's been working at it since he was at school in part-time jobs and worked for a large family butchery before going out on his own.

Ryan has seen an opportunity to use both his knowledge of meat and the growing move towards careful sourcing of ingredients among restaurants. Ten years ago I was looking for good, pasture-reared beef by trying to find farmers I could go to direct. Now there's Ryan Boon.

He's become a sort of middle-man for the chefs. He does the work of finding small or alternative producers who are raising their livestock in sustainable and humane ways. I trust him to find me beautiful beef from producers like Brenaissance in the Devon Valley. Veld-reared lamb, range-fed pigs, hunted venison; he's listened to all the catch-phrases chefs in the Western Cape are using, and gone out looking for the best of the bunch.

His connection with suppliers goes beyond just buying and re-selling the produce. In his relationship with Brenaissance, he is talking to the farmer about the animals and their care, suggesting points of improvement from a butcher's perspective. He even passes on requests and ideas from chefs where it may improve yield or change methods in husbandry. When he arrives at the back door with a cut of beef, he knows the entire history and provenance of the animal it came from.

This is one of those occasions where building relationships really pays off. In Ryan, I have a supplier I can phone and discuss ideas with. We can come up with a use for an unusual cut. We speak the same language and his knowledge of butchering, meat and availability from small producers feeds into what we do in the kitchen at Jordan.

Aged Angus Beef Tartare, Roasted Marrow, Porcini Dressing & Brioche

Tartar

200 g Angus sirloin
3 shallots
5 small gherkins
8 capers
2 g parsley
2 g chives
2 egg yolks
salt and pepper to taste

Fineley chop the beef into small even dice.

Dice the shallots, gherkins, capers and herbs and add to the meat.

Add the egg yolk to this and season with salt and pepper.

Marrow

6 marrow bones with
   the marrow removed
milk

Blanch the marrow in boiling milk for 2 minutes, then plunge into iced water.

Slice each marrow into 3–4 pieces and place on a tray. Grill under a salamander or grill with a little salt and pepper to taste.

Porcini Dressing

20 g porcini
2 cloves garlic
10 ml ponzu
30 ml extra virgin olive oil
salt and pepper to taste

Dice the porcini into 1-cm blocks and gently fry in olive oil, add 2 cloves of crushed garlic and cook out.

Remove from the heat and add the ponzu, then the olive oil, season this mix with salt and pepper to taste.

We serve the tartar stuffed into the marrow bones and garnish with the marrow and porcini dressing on top. We also crumb and fry marrow and add this for texture.

Brioche is a sweetened enriched bread and is great toasted with tartare (recipe on page 98).

Serves 4

Aged Devon Valley Boran Sirloin, Soft Herb Crust, Heirloom Tomato & Charred Aubergine

The Boran beef we use comes from Brenaissance farm in the Devon Valley. Boran is a breed normally from East Africa. The cattle are pasture-reared and free from hormones or additives. When buying beef, look for a good colour in the meat and fat, and a good marbling through the meat.

Beef

220 g sirloin
salt and pepper to taste
olive oil
butter
garlic
rosemary

Heat a non-stick pan or a skillet until smoking hot.

Season the meat with salt and pepper.

Add a little oil to the pan and sear both sides of the sirloin, getting a good caramelisation.

Add a knob of butter, crushed garlic and rosemary and put in a hot oven, 180°C, for 2 minutes. When it comes out of the oven put the herb crust on top.

Leave to rest, then slice.

Herb Crust

30 g basil
30 g parsley
10 g sage
50 g soft butter
2 cloves of garlic
salt and pepper to taste
30 g grated Parmesan

Blend all ingredients to a smooth paste, spread thinly between 2 sheets of greaseproof paper and chill.

When chilled, cut into steak-sized sheets.

Charred Aubergine Purée

30 g brown lentils
1 large aubergine
50 g crème fraîche
salt and pepper to taste

Boil the lentils until soft, char the aubergine directly on a gas flame or fire.

Once the aubergine is cooked place all ingredients in a blender and blend into a smooth paste.

Confit Heirloom Tomato

black heirloom tomato
1 clove garlic
50 ml olive oil
salt and pepper
1 bunch basil

Blanch and peel the tomatoes, place them in a pot with the oil, crushed garlic, salt, pepper and basil. Heat this to 60°C for 3 hours.

Serves 4

Penny Verburg's Suckling Pig 'Porchetta' Sunday Lunch

Penny and Niels Verburg are most famous for the wine that they produce. Luddite Shiraz has always been on my restaurant wine list and I must say I enjoy the odd bottle every now and then. They also have pigs on their farm, more for their own use but occasionally I will get a call from Niels to inform me that he has a few suckling pigs. When this happens I buy a couple and more often than not serve them for Sunday lunch. This proves to be very popular with our guests. One pig will feed around 12–15 people, so this is a great one for a gathering of friends and family.

1 suckling pig

Remove the head and trotters from the pig. We brine these and use them for other dishes.

Debone the pig, keeping the skin intact. Remove the legs and shoulders from the skin. You should now have a rectangle of pork skin with the loins attached.

Remove the meat from the shoulder, cut into large dice and gently fry in butter to cook.

Remove the meat from the legs and mince on a coarse setting.

300 g sourdough bread
100 g dried cranberries
100 g pitted prunes
1 egg
salt and pepper
1 bunch rosemary

Dice the sourdough and soak in water.

To make the stuffing, add the cranberries, prunes, diced shoulder meat and the egg to the mince. Squeeze the water out of the bread and add to the mince, season with salt, pepper and some chopped rosemary.

Lay this stuffing in the middle of the skin and roll up. Tie the pig with string to make an even shape and rest for 1 day before cooking.

Season the pork skin with lots of salt. Place the roast on some root vegetables in a hot oven, first at 220°C for half an hour and then for 1 more hour at 180°C.

Serve with some of the stuffed mushrooms (see page 162) or the honey root vegetables (see page 175).

Serves 12–15

Poached Fairview Lamb Loin, New Season's Peas, Carrot Purée & Honeyed Carrots

A celebration of spring, young lamb, peas and carrots are a classic combination.

Lamb

500 ml chicken stock
salt and pepper to taste
1 stick rosemary
1 clove garlic crushed
1 lamb loin cleaned
  and trimmed

Season the stock with the salt, pepper, rosemary and garlic and bring to a gentle simmer.

Make sure the lamb loin is clean of all sinew and fat and season with salt and pepper.

We poach the loin at 70°C, but you can heat the stock up to just below boiling and switch it off, then place the loin into the stock and leave for 10 minutes.

Check occasionally to make sure it does not overcook.

We like to serve the lamb medium rare to medium. Once it is cooked, remove from the stock and slice as required.

Carrot Purée

250 g large carrots
50 g butter
2 star anise
1 stick cinnamon
3 cardamom pods
5 g grated ginger
100 ml cream

Peel and thinly slice the carrots, then sauté them in a pot with the butter and spices. Cook this until the carrots are well cooked.

Add the cream and simmer for 2 minutes, season with salt and pepper, then blend until smooth, chill this quickly and reserve until needed.

Carrot Dressing

250 ml carrot juice
1 star anise
1 cardamom
5 g white mustard seeds
50 ml olive oil

Reduce the carrot juice with the star anise and cardamom until syrup.

Remove from the heat and strain.

Add the mustard seeds to soak and then emulsify with the olive oil.

Honeyed carrots

12 baby carrots
50 ml honey
50 ml butter

We use 2–3 baby carrots per portion and roast them in butter and honey.

Place 50 ml honey and 50 g butter into a frying pan and caramelise this until golden brown. Add the carrots and cook for 5 minutes or until the carrots are just tender. Remove the carrots from the caramel once cooked, as it will set.

Peas

When peas are fresh they are sweet and crunchy. Simply plunge them in boiling water for 20 seconds, then into an ice bath.

We peel off the outer skin but you may feel that this is not necessary.

Serves 4

Roasted Rack of Fairview Lamb, Roasted Kidney, Liver & Parsley Sauce

Lamb

1 8-bone rack of lamb
4 herb crust recipe
(see page 128)
200 g lamb liver
2 lamb kidneys

At the restaurant, we use pasture-reared lamb which mostly come from Fairview. Ask your butcher to French trim and chime the rack – this will make it easier to portion.

Score and render down the fat on the lamb rack, then roast in a hot oven at 180°C for 4–5 minutes.

Once roasted, place the herb crust onto the fat and leave to rest.

We first pan fry the kidneys in butter, then roast them with a sour dough crumb on them, which is a mixture of sour dough, parsley, anchovies and garlic.

Coat the liver in flour before searing in foaming butter. This is very quick, no more than 1 minute each side.

Parsley Sauce

50 g parsley
2 g salted lemon
3 anchovy
1 clove garlic
1 tsp Dijon mustard
100 ml olive oil
salt and pepper to taste

Place all ingredients into a blender and blend until smooth.

Season to taste and refrigerate until ready to use.

Serves 4

Pan-roasted Beef Sweetbreads, Creamed Porcini & Turnips

Sweetbreads are the thymus and pancreas glands from animals. Mostly beef and lamb sweetbreads are eaten these days. Sweetbreads have an irresistible flavour – best served lightly dusted with flour and fried in butter.

Sweetbreads

400 g sweetbreads
flour for dusting
300 g butter
5 g rosemary
2 cloves garlic, crushed
salt and pepper to taste

Blanch the sweetbreads in boiling water for 30 seconds, and then plunge into iced water to cool.

Peel off any pieces of fat and sinew from the outside, dry the cleaned sweetbreads and refrigerate.

To cook the sweetbreads, dust them in seasoned flour and pan fry in butter, rosemary and garlic until golden on both sides. Then roast them in a hot oven at 180°C for 8 minutes.

Pickled Turnip

1 large turnip
salt
1 cup white wine vinegar
3 tbsp sugar
½ cup water

Peel and thinly slice the large turnip.

Sprinkle a little salt over the slices and allow to sit in a colander for 20 minutes. This will help draw out any excess water. After 20 minutes, rinse in water and dry.

Boil the vinegar, sugar and water and then pour over the sliced turnip.

Roasted Baby Turnip

1 bunch baby turnips
200 g butter

Wash and trim the baby turnips. Place 200 g of butter into a pot and melt slowly, add the baby turnips and poach in the butter until soft and tender. This may take 1–2 hours.

Porcini Cream

300 g porcini
2 shallots chopped
6 gloves garlic crushed
1 glass white wine
250 ml chicken stock
250 ml cream

Brush the porcini clean and cut into small dice.

Sauté the shallots and garlic in a little butter until translucent. Add the porcini and cook gently for a further 5 minutes.

Deglaze with white wine and reduce by half. Add the chicken stock and again reduce by half. Add the cream and reduce until it has a saucy consistency.

Serves 4

Pickled Glen Oaks Pork Fillet

Glen Oaks is at the top of the Hemel an Aarde valley, the pigs roam free eating what pigs should eat and doing what pigs should do.

1 pig cheek
1 pork fillet
200 ml white wine vinegar
100 g sugar
100 ml water
salt and pepper taste
100 g course salt
3 large onions
1 bulb garlic
10 g tarragon
3 star anise
3 cardamom pods

Trim the pork cheek of any sinew, then cover with the coarse salt and cure. After 6 hours, wash off the salt and cold smoke until intensely flavored.

Cut the onions in half, crush the garlic and place on a baking dish. Put the cheek onto this and bake for 4 hours at 150°C. Once cooked, wrap in plastic warp and press to set.

Trim the pork fillet of any sinew. Heat the vinegar, sugar and water with the cardamom, tarragon and star anise in. As soon as it boils pour over the fillet, cover and allow to cool.

Slice the pork fillet into thin medallions and season with salt and pepper. Slice the pork cheek on a meat slicer.

Mustard Chantilly

20 g wholegrain mustard
50 g crème fraîche
200 ml whipped cream
salt and pepper to taste

Work the mustard into the crème fraîche, then fold in the whipped cream and season.

Green Sauce

1 shallot
10 g parsley
5 g mint
5 g chives
5 g basil
2 cloves garlic
lemon zest
3 anchovies
50 ml olive oil

Place all ingredients in a blender and work to a smooth paste.

Serves 10

Vegetables

"How are you today Steve?" It's always my first question when I'm on the phone to Steve Botha. "Like Magic," has always been his answer.

I first started using Magic Herbs when I opened Jardine Restaurant in Cape Town. Every Thursday his bakkie would pull up outside, just before service, and it was always overflowing with the most amazing produce. There'd be pencil-thin baby leeks, golden and candy-stripe beets, elderflowers and a whole bunch more. All of it was grown in his huge back garden in Porterville.

I was once invited to prepare a launch dinner for the Design Indaba at the Castle in Cape Town. I called in Steve and Sue Baker from Wild Peacock, and we set up an interactive marketplace for Indaba invitees to show exactly how high the standard of South African produce can be.

Steve set up a live garden using baby vegetables, herbs and Jerusalem artichoke plants, and my dish was designed to showcase how important good produce is. People were just fascinated by Steve's produce and enthralled by his passion and many, many stories.

As a chef, it's a pleasure to meet someone who gets excited to the point of being fanatical about produce. Steve has been instrumental in working with chefs and developing many vegetable products that seem common-place these days. Once chefs were using his unusual or heritage vegetables or micro-greens, it follows that the big grocery retailers were going to cotton on. So, the fact that you can find micro-herbs and other interesting produce at the shops is in some small way thanks to Steve Botha and growers like him.

An important note on buying and cooking vegetables is that fresh is best. As soon as a vegetable is picked, its quality and goodness slowly diminish. Homegrown is always first prize. Failing that, buy from the grower – there are many small producers who need our support.

Salad of Organic Baby Beets, Buffalo-milk Mozzarella, Orange & Vanilla

500 ml freshly squeezed
  orange juice
1 vanilla pod
2 star anise
3 cardamom pods
250 g baby beetroot
100 g buffalo-milk mozzarella
1 ball buffalo-milk yoghurt
1 egg
50 g breadcrumbs
50 ml olive oil
salt and pepper to taste
150 g watercress
10g fennel leaf
5 g toasted pumpkin seeds

Put the orange juice into a pot with the vanilla pod, star anise and cardamom. Reduce this until a thick glaze. Strain off the spices and chill.

Roast the beetroots in a tin foil bag at 180°C for 30 minutes or until cooked. Peel while still hot and leave to cool.

Tear the mozzarella into pieces. You will need 6 pieces per plate, 3 of which we coat in the egg, then bread crumb and deep fry. The other 3 we dress with olive oil and season with salt and pepper.

Garnish the dish with toasted pumpkin seeds, fennel leaves and some watercress.

Serves 4

Beetroot Tart, Horseradish Cream, Pickled Aubergine, Shimeji & Aged Balsamic

A Jardine favourite. Even today people come to Jordan and ask for the beetroot tart. I was cooking at the Good Food Show in 2006 and had to compete against another chef while coming up with dishes from ingredients available before us. Puff pastry, beetroot, crème fraîche and horseradish were on the table and this dish popped into my head.
We prepared this dish for 600 people on the side of Table Mountain at the Table of Peace and Unity. Jerome Peters, my sous chef then, Andrew Baker Boy and myself worked through the night in the Mount Nelson kitchen as Jardine's was not big enough. What a long night!

Pastry

250 g butter puff pastry

On a floured surface, roll out the puff pastry as thin as you can get it. Cut this into 12-cm squares, dust off any excess flour and refrigerate.

Heat a large non-stick frying pan. Add a little olive oil and fry the pastry until it is golden brown on both sides. Occasionally press down the air bubbles to keep flat.

Beetroot

1 large beetroot

Wrap the beetroot in tin foil and bake at 180 °C for 30–40 minutes. Once it is cooked, peel and cool down.

Pickled Aubergine and Shimeji

50 ml water
50 g sugar
100 ml white wine vinegar
1 medium aubergine
1 packet shimeji mushrooms

Heat the water, sugar and vinegar in a pot. Peel the aubergine and cut into 1-cm squares, trim the shimeji into individual mushrooms.

Bring the pickling liquid up to the boil and pour over the aubergine and shimeji.

Cover this immediately and leave to cool.

Horseradish Cream

50 g fresh horseradish or a
  small jar horseradish cream
100 ml crème fraîche
salt and pepper to taste

Mix the horseradish cream with the crème fraîche
and season with salt and pepper.

To Serve

5 ml aged balsamic vinegar
salt and pepper to taste
25 g chopped chives

Slice the beetroot very thin on a mandolin or with
a sharp knife.

Spread each puff pastry tart with crème fraîche
mix and lay on the beetroot. Trim the tarts into
perfect squares.

Drain off the required amount of aubergine and
mushroom and dress with olive oil, aged balsamic,
salt, pepper and chopped chives.

Spoon around a little of the dressing and serve.

Makes 4 tarts

Confit Heirloom Aubergine, Heirloom Tomato, Buffalo-milk Labneh, Basil & Green Olive Tapenade

1 large heirloom aubergine
250 g small heirloom tomatoes
50 g basil
1 bulb garlic
500 ml extra virgin olive oil
salt and pepper to taste

Peel the aubergine and cut into dice, a similar size to the tomato. Blanch and peel the tomato and place in a pot with the aubergine, half of the basil and 2 cloves of garlic.

Cover with olive oil and season with salt and pepper. Heat this to 60°C and leave for 3–4 hours.

100 g green olives
4 anchovies

Place the green olives, 4 cloves of garlic and anchovies in a blender and blend until smooth. Add some olive oil if necessary and season.

250 g buffalo-milk yoghurt
1 lemon
5 g chives to garnish

Hang the yoghurt in a cheesecloth and let the moisture drip out. Leave this overnight for the best result, then finely grate the zest from the lemon and add with some salt and pepper to taste.

Roll the labneh into balls and store covered in olive oil.

To serve, we brown the aubergine a little in a hot pan. This also helps to extract any excess oil.

This is great as a vegetarian starter or as an accompaniment to grilled fish or meat.

Serves 4

Jerusalem Artichoke Purée, Buttered Fettuccini, Ashed Goat's Cheese & Nasturtiums

One year at Jordan I planted a row of Jerusalem artichokes from a few we had left over in the kitchen. What a harvest we got from that one row – lots of delicious tubers to cook with. The next year even more sprouted up and almost took over the whole garden. Be warned if you plant Jerusalem artichokes – make sure you dig every one of them out or you will have millions.

Artichoke Purée

150 g Jerusalem artichoke
100 g butter
6 shallots chopped
6 cloves garlic chopped
1 litre chicken stock
250 ml cream
100 g Parmesan
salt and pepper to taste

Wash and scrub the Jerusalem artichokes, making sure they are free of any soil. Leave 5–6 whole for the garnish – the remainder can be sliced up for cooking.

In a large sauce pan heat the butter until foaming, then add the sliced Jerusalem artichokes, shallots and garlic. Sauté this on a gentle heat until the Jerusalem artichokes are well caramelised. This will take around 1 hour.

When they are caramelised, you can add in the chicken stock and simmer for 1 more hour.

Add the cream and Parmesan, season with salt and pepper and then blend until smooth.

Pasta

400 g flour
300 g egg yolks
pinch of salt
10 ml olive oil

We make our own pasta – it really does make a difference in the end – but you need a pasta machine, the right flour and time. You can buy a good egg-based dried pasta, which will work as well.

Combine all ingredients to form a stiff dough and work until smooth.

This dough needs to be rested for at least 1 hour before rolling. We roll out on the machine, starting at the lowest setting and gradually getting thinner and thinner. Fold the pasta in half and roll through a few times to laminate it – this way you get a better end product.

If you do make your own pasta, you can dry it until needed or on cooking. Make sure your water is boiling with a little salt. Plunge the pasta in for no more than 2 minutes – fresh pasta cooks very quickly.

To Serve

1 hard ashed goat's cheese
nasturtiums for garnish

Slice the artichokes very thinly on a mandolin or even with a vegetable peeler.

Blanch these briefly in milk, then dry on paper.

Fry these in hot oil until crispy – they are a great garnish and add a level of texture to the dish.

Grate a generous amount of the ashed goat's cheese over the pasta when you serve.

Garnish with nasturtiums.

Braised Lettuce, Mushroom & Feta

This is a quick and easy side, a great accompaniment to a steak, some grilled fish, or the suckling pig.

2 heads baby cos lettuce
5 g basil
5 g parsley
6 large brown mushrooms
extra virgin olive oil
100 g buffalo-milk feta
salt and pepper to taste

Slice and wash the cos lettuce. Chop and add the herbs, dress with a little olive oil, crumble in the feta and season.

Dress the mushrooms with a little olive oil and season. Fill up the mushrooms with the lettuce and grill in a hot oven for 10–15 minutes.

New Season's Baby Carrots, Carrot Cake Purée, Buffalo-milk Mozzarella & Herbs

The first carrots of the season are the best. Tender, juicy and straight from the ground, they are full of goodness. You don't even have to peel them – just wash and scrub with a sponge to remove any soil. For a starter you can work on 4–5 baby carrots per person but this also makes a great summer salad accompaniment to roasted lamb or fish.

Baby Carrots

250 ml vegetable stock
2 sprigs thyme
50 g butter
1 garlic, crushed
2 bunches baby carrots
zest and juice of 1 orange

Heat the stock, thyme, butter and garlic.

Scrub the carrots clean and trim off any excess leaves. Reserve some carrots to use for the crudités.

Simply slice the carrot thinly – you can even use a peeler to get a uniform thickness – and place in iced water to crisp up.

Add the carrots to the stock and bring to the boil, then turn down the heat and cook gently for 4–5 minutes. Once cooked to your liking, turn off the heat and leave to cool down in the stock.

Carrot Cake Purée

2 cloves garlic crushed
3 shallots sliced
3 large carrots peeled and
    grated
1 stick cinnamon
1 star anise
1 cardamom pod
100 g butter
50 ml chicken stock
50 ml cream

Sauté the garlic, shallots, carrots and spices in butter until well cooked. Try not to caramelise this too much. We tie the spices up in a muslin cloth, as it is easier to remove when blending.

Once the carrot is almost cooked, add the chicken stock and reduce by half. Then add the cream and reduce this by half. Remove the spices and blend into a smooth purée.

Carrot Dressing

250 ml carrot juice
1 tsp brown sugar
1 tsp sherry vinegar
50 ml olive oil
½ teaspoon of white mustard
seeds soaked in a little white
  wine vinegar

Reduce the carrot juice and sugar by 2/3 until it starts to becomes a little sticky.

Remove from the heat and add the vinegar.

Emulsify this in a blender with the olive oil, then add the soaked mustard seeds.

The mustard seeds add a spicy taste and nice crunch to the dressing.

Buffalo-milk Mozzarella

We use Wayne's mozzarella in many dishes. I like mozzarella for its subtle flavour, but more for its silky texture. 1 ball of mozzarella should be enough for 4–6 people. Tear the mozzarella and dress with olive oil, salt and pepper. For this dish we also crumb some and deep fry.

To garnish this dish we use wild herbs that we pick on the farm such as nasturtium, chickweed, woodsorrel and purslane. You could try to find some wild herbs or use watercress or baby spinach.

Serves 4

Spicy Kale, Honeyed Parsnip & 'Kaaings'

This is a very tasty starter salad or could be used as a side for roast lamb or duck. I am in love with kale. It has a great earthy taste, wonderful texture and is very good for you. I love serving it raw as in this dish or lightly braised with a bit of garlic and chicken stock.

500 g parsnips
50 g honey
50 g butter
400 g kale
1 bulb garlic
100 ml spicy dressing (see the
   oyster recipe on page 59)
25 g finely chopped parsley
25 g finely chopped chives

First of all, peel and dice the parsnips. Place them in a large pot, cover with water and boil until tender.

Blend with the honey and butter until very smooth. Taste to see if there is enough honey, otherwise add more. Be careful not to make it too sweet.

Wash the kale, then cut into fine julienne. We roll the leaves up together like you are making a cigar then slice with a sharp knife. Keep the kale in iced water so that it is nice and crunchy.

Slice the garlic thinly on a mandolin and poach gently in milk. Repeat this process once with fresh milk. You are not trying to cook the garlic, just remove some of the bitter oils.

Drain the garlic on a paper towel, then fry in vegetable oil at 160°C until light golden brown and crispy.

To serve, drain off the kale and remove as much water as possible – a salad spinner will work the best.

Place a base of the parsnip purée onto your serving plate, the parsnip will help cool the burn from the spicy kale. Dress the kale with the spicy dressing and fresh herbs and place on top of the purée. Garnish with the garlic chips to add a little salty crunch.

Serves 4

Wild

Every year Louise's dad goes hunting at a place in the Northern Cape owned by a mate of his. How it got its name is a bit hazy for me, but the guys all call it *Skroef.*

It's a huge place, 13-thousand hectares on the Orange River with no internal fences and a couple of natural hot springs. Every time he goes, he asks me what I want and the answer is always the same: "A gemsbok."

Getting a whole, hunted antelope into the restaurant is one of the highlights of the winter season for me. It goes back to what cooking is all about. Like our emphasis on technique, I think it's important for the kitchen crew to learn where all the cuts of meat come from. It also allows us to connect very directly with where food comes from.

Butchering an animal on the pass in the restaurant is quite an event for us. It's messy and it's very visual, but it's also a great team-building exercise. Everyone gets involved. There's cutting and carrying and holding and hoisting. All of this brings us together with a single purpose, and I think that each crew member goes away with a new appreciation of their craft.

We do the obvious things with the choice cuts like fillets, loins and shoulders, but we try to use everything we can. Livers, sweetbreads, kidneys, shanks, shins, there's some use for all of it in a creative kitchen. There will always be a new idea too: Ciska might want to cure some cuts, or Dale suggest making a salami. The idea is to push boundaries and do justice to the sacrifice of the animal.

Braised Springbok Shank, Honeyed Winter Roots & Cauliflower Purée

A real hearty winter meal, I love the rich gelatinous flavour you get from braising shanks.

Braised Springbok Shank

6 springbok shanks
50 g carrot, diced
50 g leek, chopped
1 onion, sliced
1 bulb garlic, crushed
thyme and rosemary
250 ml red wine
3 litres chicken stock
10 g parsley
salt and pepper
1 cup of flour for dusting
  the shanks
100 g net fat

In order to get nice even fat springbok shanks, we braise 6 to give us 4.

Sauté the vegetables, then deglaze with the red wine.

Reduce this by half, then add the chicken stock and bring up to the boil.

Season and flour the springbok shanks, then brown in a hot pan and add to the braising liquid.

Gently braise the shanks until soft. This will take time so be patient.

When cooked, remove the springbok from the stock and remove all the meat from the bone. Select 4 of the nice thin bones for our re-made shanks.

Season the meat and add a little chopped parsley. Shape into 4 balls.

Place the nice bone into the ball of meat and wrap this in the net fat.

Shape back into a shank shape and chill until needed.

Strain and reduce the braising liquid. This will be the base for our sauce and help glaze the shanks.

Heat a large non-stick pan and add a little butter.

Gently sauté the springbok shanks, being careful not to break the net fat.

Add the reduced sauce and baste the shanks. Place into a hot oven and heat through, basting constantly to get a nice glaze.

Cauliflower Purée

1 potato
1 small cauliflower
1 litre milk
50 g Parmesan
salt and pepper to taste

Peel and dice the potato, chop the cauliflower into small pieces, then boil in the milk with the potato.

Once the potato is soft, drain off the milk and blend with the Parmesan and seasoning.

Honeyed Root Vegetables

50 g butter
50 g honey
assorted root vegetables

Root vegetables are delicious roasted with honey. I think the earthy flavour is complimented by the rich sweetness of the honey. Parsnips, carrot, celeriac, fennel, turnip and kohlrabi are all great winter vegetables that would work for this dish.

First peel and cut the root vegetables into similar sizes.

Heat the butter and honey in a non-stick pan until it begins to caramelise.

Add the vegetables, making sure they are all well coated in the honey butter, then bake in a hot oven for 10 minutes or until soft.

Serves 4

Double-herbed Springbok, Confit Celeriac, Braised Savoy Cabbage & Caraway

Springbok

600 g springbok loin
5 g thyme
5 g rosemary
50 g net fat

Clean any sinew from the springbok loin, then portion onto 150 g portions and season with salt and pepper.

Fineley chop the thyme and rosemary leaves and season the springbok with it.

Lay out the net fat into a square that will wrap the springbok loin twice.

Roll the springbok loin in the fat, trim the edges and refrigerate.

To cook the springbok, heat a non-stick pan on a gentle heat and add a knob of butter.

Slowly pan fry the loin until it is caramelised evenly, then roast in an oven at 180°C for 2–3 minutes.

Allow to rest for 5 minutes before cutting.

Keep the springbok medium rare as it becomes very dry when cooked more.

Celeriac

1 celeriac
1 litre milk
salt and pepper to taste
500 g duck fat

Peel the celeriac and cut 4 rectangular blocks for the confit and dice up the remainder to make celeriac purée.

Place the diced celeriac in a pot with the milk.

Boil this until the celeriac is soft, then drain off the milk and blend until smooth. Season this with salt and pepper. Cool down until required.

Place the rectangular blocks into a small pot with the duck fat and confit just below boiling until soft. This will take around 1 hour.

Cabbage

1 Savoy cabbage
50 g butter
3 shallots sliced
3 cloves crushed garlic
5 g caraway seeds
salt and pepper to taste
parsley
4 rashers pancetta

Remove 4 of the green outer leaves and blanch them in salted boiling water.

Refresh the leaves in iced water – you want them to be vibrant green.

Shred the remainder of the cabbage and sauté in butter with the shallot, garlic and caraway seeds.

Season this well with salt and pepper and add some chopped parsley.

Cut the blanched outer leaves with a cutter and stuff each leaf with the shredded cabbage.

Wrap into a ball with cling film.

Place this in a pot of boiling water to heat up, remove the cling film before serving.

Serves 4

Pan-roasted Gemsbok Loin,
Poached Forelle Pear & Honeyed Parsnip

Cooking any loin of venison seems to be quite daunting for a home cook, but it is actually quite easy and should not cause too much stress. The secret, if there is one, is that once it is sealed nicely, a gentle heat in the oven will give the best results.

Gemsbok Loin

150 g gemsbok loin
  per portion
salt and pepper to taste
30g butter
1 stick rosemary
3 cloves garlic chopped
  with the skin

You can substitute the gemsbok for most other small game loins as the loins of most animals cook the same. I prefer the flavour of gemsbok.

Season the meat with salt and pepper then brown it in a hot non-stick pan.

When it has an even colour add the butter, rosemary and garlic and cook for 2 minutes in an oven set to 160°C.

After 2 minutes, remove from the oven and cover with plastic wrap to rest. After 5 minutes resting, the loin is ready to serve.

Poached Pear

4 pears
250 ml red wine
3 cardamom pods
3 star anise
zest of 1 orange
1 vanilla pod
200 ml water
200 g sugar

Peel the pears and remove the core with a scoop.

Place all other ingredients into a large pot and bring to the boil. Add the pears and poach gently until soft. Once the pears are cooked, allow them to cool in the liquid.

Serves 4

Seared Gemsbok Liver, Poached Pear,
Celeriac Purée, Hazelnut & Celeriac Dressing

1 gemsbok liver – we use
   150 g per portion

Ask your butcher to remove the skin from the liver, then cut into 150-g portions.

Heat a non-stick pan and add a little oil and a knob of butter.

Let the butter begin to foam, then add the liver.

Sauté this for 1 minute on both sides, remove from the pan and allow to rest.

Poached Pear

1 Forelle pear
250 ml red wine
3 cardamom pods
3 star anise
100 g sugar

Peel and core the pear. Place the red wine, cardamom, star anise and sugar into a pot.

Add the pear and poach for 1–2 hours.

Once it is cooked, leave to cool in the liquid until required. We slice the pear thinly and arrange onto the plate.

Celeriac Purée and Celeriac for dressing

1 celeriac
500 ml milk

Peel the celeriac – we will use 20 g per person.

For the dressing this is diced into small blocks and poached in duck fat, you could use olive oil.

Dice the remainder and place in a pot with the milk.

Boil this until the celeriac is soft, then drain off the milk and blend until smooth. Season this with salt and pepper.

Cool until required.

Hazelnut dressing

Toast the hazelnuts in a hot oven until golden brown, then crush lightly.

Mix the olive oil with the sherry vinegar, add the hazelnuts and diced celeriac and season with salt and pepper.

We slice the pear into thin strips then arrange the liver around it.

We serve a little gemsbok ragout with it – this is trimmings from the shoulder, braised until it breaks down. Be generous with the dressing and celeriac purée.

Serves 4

Chocolate

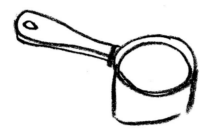

Who doesn't love chocolate? It makes you feel good. It makes you want more. It's always the pictures of some chocolatey treat in a magazine that get you thinking about food. That's why we use a lot of it in desserts, because it is such an indulgent treat. Most of the recipes in this section call for 70% dark chocolate, and we usually use a French brand called Valrhona. The percentage marked on chocolate refers to the proportion of cocoa mass in the product. If the percentage gets too high, the bitter note climbs and the sweetness diminishes. Around 70% works for us.

As you can imagine, we use lots of chocolate at The Bakery at Jordan. We opened the bakery in December 2013, because I've always had an interest in baking. As with the Bree Street restaurant, it wasn't going to be long before we opened one at Jordan.

Everything in the bakery is hand-made. The artisan breads are baked in a huge wood-fired oven that burns alien trees as fuel. As with the restaurant and everything we do, we take the time to source the best natural products available. We use biodynamic stone ground flour, homegrown olives from the farm, fruit for jam from the farm next door, great coffee and local craft beers. The crowd favourite in the daily pastry display is the chocolate salted caramel tart.

When we opened it, Louise moved over from the restaurant to manage the bakery operation. There's a bit of a joke among regulars, that there are: "lots of Louises on Jordan". Louise is joined by Louise Starey who runs front of house there.

Ciska, Roystarr and Speedy do all the baking, as well as handling the small breakfast and lunch menu where guests can enjoy the more casual side of the Jordan food and wine experience.

White Chocolate Torte

This dessert came about after I was requested to prepare the dessert course for the Eat Out Awards dinner for 500 people. I had in mind to prepare a rich luscious chocolate torte for the guests to savour after their main meal.

Torte

250 g white chocolate
200 g butter
6 egg yolks
50 g castor sugar
50 g cake flour
100 ml cream

Preheat the oven to 150°C.

Melt the chocolate and butter over a double boiler.

Combine the egg yolks and sugar but do not incorporate any air into the mixture – use a spatula or spoon to mix.

Combine the chocolate and egg mixture. Then fold in the flour and cream.

Bake in a shallow tray for 15 minutes until it just starts to set.

Leave to set in the fridge, then portion as desired.

Raspberry Purée

6–8 raspberries per person
250 ml Noble Late Harvest dessert wine (we use Jordan Mellifera)

Soak the raspberries in the wine for 12 hours.

Drain before serving.

Raspberry Sorbet

600 ml water
100 g glucose
175 g sugar
300 g raspberry purée
1 lemon juiced

Bring the water, sugar and glucose to the boil, add the raspberry purée and cool over an ice bath.

Add lemon juice to taste.

Churn in an ice cream machine and freeze.

Serves 4

Chocolate & Hazelnut Royaltine

There a few steps to making this recipe, but if you are organised and have everything ready, it is straightforward. Temperature is the key to success so make sure the chocolate is not too hot when you fold in the cream. For years at Jardine we could not get Fueilletine (crispy biscuit) in South Africa, so we used crushed Frosties, which was a good alternative.

Base

40 g butter
100 g milk chocolate
120 g praline
120 g Fueilletine

Line the container or cake tin with greaseproof paper.

Melt the butter, chocolate and praline, then fold in the Fueilletine – do not let this mixture get cold.

Cover the base of your tin with the mixture as evenly and thinly as possible.

Once it is in the container, you can put it in the fridge to set.

Mousse

120 g dark chocolate, 70%
120 g milk chocolate, 46%
120 g praline
280 g cream
200 g whipped cream

Place the chocolate and praline in a large bowl.

Scald the cream (bring to the boil) and pour it over the chocolate and praline to melt them.

The chocolate should be a nice temperature to fold in the whipped cream (it should be less than body temperature). Do not overwork it – fold it just until it is completely incorporated.

Pour this mix over the crispy base and place in the fridge to set.

Dark Chocolate Glaze

150 g sugar
300 g water
66 g cocoa powder, 100%
138 g cream
4 gelatin leaves

Place all ingredients, apart from the gelatin, into a pot and bring to the boil. Remove from the heat and add the soaked gelatin.

Leave this to cool. Then pour a thin layer over the mousse.

Refrigerate until completely set, remove from the mould and divide into portions.

This is delicious with fresh berries and a vanilla or white chocolate ice cream.

Serves 4

Chocolate Caramel Tart

Pâte Sablée

250 g cake flour
200 g icing sugar
200 g butter
4 egg yolks

Mix the sifted flour and icing sugar.

Cut the butter into cubes and rub into the flour until it is a sandy texture.

Gradually incorporate the egg yolks to form dough.

Refrigerate for 2 hours before use.

Roll out the pastry and line the tart moulds and blind bake until golden brown.

Salted Caramel

50 g butter
50 g castor sugar
25 ml cream
Maldon sea salt

Melt the butter and castor sugar and caramelise to golden brown.

Add the cream to stop the cooking process and pour a thin layer into each baked tart. Sprinkle the caramel with sea salt.

Chocolate Ganache

250 ml cream
300 g dark chocolate, 70%
2 egg yolks

Bring the cream to the boil and pour over the chocolate to melt.

Once completely melted, add the egg yolks and pour into the tarts.

Leave to set for 1 hour.

Makes 8 tarts

Chocolate & Orange Terrine

450 g dark chocolate, 70%
150 g cream
1 orange zest
4 egg yolks
250 g crème fraîche

Melt the chocolate over a double boiler then pour over the scalded cream. Add the egg yolks one at a time, then fold in the crème fraîche and orange zest.

Genoise Sponge

4 eggs
125 g sugar
125 g cake flour
50 g melted butter

Whisk the eggs and sugar in a mixing machine until thick. Fold in the flour and butter, then spread out on grease proof paper and bake at 180°C for 8 minutes.

Remove from the oven and cut the same size as the mould.

To assemble the terrine, make alternate layers of chocolate ganache and sponge. Press the terrine and refrigerate.

Butterscotch Sauce

100 g butter
100 g sugar
100 ml cream

Caramelise the butter and sugar until dark golden brown, then remove from the heat and add the cream. Bring to the boil, then chill.

Candid Zest

Zest 2 oranges, then boil the zest for 1 minute. Boil again in fresh water and repeat this process 3 times. Leave to dry completely, then coat in sugar.

Makes a 1 kg terrine mould

Crew

As much as the standard of a restaurant can be judged by the effort and knowledge used to procure and prepare the best ingredients, it is nothing without its staff. They add the human dimension.

Our team builds the relationships with our customers, so we expect a lot of them. Regulars often know them by name, sharing a joke or a quick chat as they arrive. From the scullers to the managers, the crew help to personalise the experience and elevate it beyond simply sitting down to a meal.

Riaan or Isabella are there to welcome and attend to any requests, while the floor is handled by Quincy, Zandi, Nikki or Cindy. They each remember different things about your previous experiences, likes or dislikes, and do their best to make your meal perfect.

In the kitchen Big Richie, Kat, Brendan, Fortune and Pepsi are all moving like a well-oiled machine, focused on getting everything right. Dale and Kyle are cracking the whip, bringing everything together to make sure it all runs smoothly.

We put a great deal of effort into selecting and training the crew. Daily briefings on the menu, regular wine tastings with Gary Jordan and robust camaraderie give them the skills and confidence to introduce their personality into your experience.

Cheese

When I was still learning to cook and working in kitchens in London, I never gave a second's thought to cheese. It really didn't feature on my radar as an important part of any meal.

That was until I worked at The Four Seasons. There was a sommelier there who would bring all kinds of cheeses into the kitchen for the chefs to taste. The guys on the line made stupid faces and farting noises when he opened the cheese, but he ignored us. He would come in with a half bottle of some wine from service and encourage us to taste it with this or that cheese. It took a while, but gradually I came to understand the beauty of cheese on a menu.

Here in the Western Cape, we are blessed with access to incredible cheesemakers. There are South African artisans who are starting to make a real mark on the international stage, taking gold medals at prestigious international awards. In 2010, Dalewood, whose Huguenot cheese is a permanent feature in the cheese room, took double gold at the World Cheese Awards in France. Other producers, like Klein River and Swissland, are getting there by leaps and bounds. We also have amazing innovators, like Buffalo Ridge Cheese with their real buffalo-milk mozzarella, who make cheese such an adventure.

Riaan and Isabella – manager and sommelier – compile the cheese boards. They discuss what we have and how it will pair with our wines, and decide on suggestions for the menu. When people ask for the cheese selection, they take them to the cheese room and offer a selection of four cheeses to round off the meal. It's a wonderful little ritual that we've become known for at Jordan.

Weltevrede Figs

The story of Weltevrede Figs is one that speaks volumes about why we search for interesting and unusual produce. It illustrates why it is better to go off in search of real, passionate producers, rather than filling in a form from a supplier and having some homogenous stuff dropped off at the back door.

We first found Weltevrede on a visit to Prince Albert in the Karoo. The town is known as a little foodie paradise, with all sorts of unique produce available. It is home to Gay's Guernsey Dairy and Karoo Gold Honey among others, but Weltevrede is an incredible story.

The farm is at the end of a dusty road through the rough landscape of the Karoo. When you think it can't go on, you come over a rise and there's suddenly a ribbon of lush green in the desert. These are their Adam fig trees. The farm has been in the family for generations, and it is run today as it was 200 years ago with no electricity and an honest hard day's work.

During harvest, you can hear the women singing as they process and dry figs, and the men in the orchards singing as they pick. It's a completely unique story for a product with an incredible heritage of love and dedication that goes into making it.

We get a green fig preserve from them to serve with the cheese boards, and jam for The Bakery. In season, we take as many fresh figs as we can get to use in the kitchen. Whenever we get a chance, we go and visit the farm. They have a couple of beautiful, original old homesteads for hire and it's all run on gas and paraffin lamps. There isn't a TV or a cellphone signal for miles – perfect for a truly artisanal product.

Index

NOTES:

NOTES:

Published by Russel Wasserfall Food,
an imprint of Jacana Media (Pty) Ltd, in 2014

Publisher and project manager
Russel Wasserfall

Editorial and advertising
Russel Wasserfall, rwasserfall@eca.co.za

Edited and photographed by Russel Wasserfall

Art directed and designed by Roxy Spears of Good Design
Illustrations by Rucita Vassen of Good Design

© Text: George Jardine, 2014
© Photos: Russel Wasserfall, 2014
© Illustrations & Design: Good Design, 2014

First published in 2014 by Jacana Media (Pty) Ltd
10 Orange Street, Sunnyside,
Auckland Park, 2092, South Africa
+27 11 628 3200, www.jacana.co.za

Printed by Craft Print, Singapore
Job no. 002308

ISBN 978-1-928247-02-9